Kaleidoscope

& other sequences

ROWAN B. FORTUNE &
JAN FORTUNE-WOOD (eds)

INDEPENDENT · INNOVATIVE · INTERNATIONAL

Published by Cinnamon Press
Meirion House
Glan yr afon
Tanygrisiau
Blaenau Ffestiniog
Gwynedd
LL41 3SU
www.cinnamonpress.com

ISBN: 978-1-907090-36-3
British Library Cataloguing in Publication Data. A CIP record for this book can be obtained from the British Library.

Designed and typeset in Palatino by Cinnamon Press. Cover design from original artwork 'Caryon Kaleidoscope' © Anna Yakimova; agency: dreamstime.com

Printed in Poland.

Cinnamon Press is represented in the UK by Inpress Ltd www.inpressbooks.co.uk and in Wales by the Welsh Books Council www.cllc.org.uk.

Cinnamon Press acknowledges the financial support of the Welsh Books Council.

Contents

Foreword
by Matthew Francis

This is a substantial anthology of sequences by twenty-five poets. It's a strong idea: the subgenre of the sequence seems to me particularly vibrant and significant at the moment, as poets look for the opportunity to write something more substantial and ambitious than the individual lyric while retaining some of the accessibility and marketability of shorter forms. I don't know of another anthology that explores this theme, and this one does an excellent job of it. It's not merely a ragbag of poems but an investigation of the many solutions the poets have found to the same problem: how to combine a number of short pieces into a longer one while keeping some sense of the independence of the constituent parts. This makes it both intriguing and genuinely informative - I felt I learned a lot from reading it.

Curiously, one approach that is not much in evidence here is sequentiality. The order the sequences are arranged in often does not seem very important, or only important for aesthetic reasons rather than narrative or chronological ones. Susan Utting's treatment of the children's game of 'Stones, Scissors, Paper', Derek Sellen's ekphrastic studies of Spanish paintings, or a more clearly fictional example like Bonnie Thurston's series of monologues by an anchorite, are all satisfyingly grouped by a particular theme, but none of them has a dynamic that pushes the reader through them from beginning to end in the way that a story or even an essay usually has. This is a feature that I think accurately reflects the handling of sequences in contemporary poetry generally. Perhaps the word itself is a misnomer and we should rename them *sets*.

The poets here include some well-known names like Alison Brackenbury, Myra Schneider and Tony Curtis, as well as many whose names were new to me. There are some interesting points of comparison. Brackenbury writes about one of the British floods of recent years, while Wendy Klein describes the aftermath of Hurricane Katrina in New Orleans; Sellen and Curtis respond to the work of artists; Pete Marshall and Bruce Ackerley both evoke the Welsh landscape. I particularly enjoyed Peter Barry's witty reminiscences of a seminary education in the 1960s and Susan Richardson's vivid recreations of Viking culture in Orkney. Part of the charm of Richardson's sequence lies in its variety of technical approaches, and this is a feature of the book generally. From Brackenbury's skilful use of traditional form to N.S. Thompson's mix of verse and prose (which reminded me of Roy Fisher's great sequence *City*) to the openly experimental cut-up style writing of Lee Duggan, this is an anthology that celebrates technical and stylistic diversity. In an age of poetic factionalism, that in itself is a strong recommendation.

Kaleidoscope

Susan Utting

Stone, Scissors, Paper

i *Stone:*

Words stick in my mouth
like crusts that want soup: water,
salt, meat, a stir with a long spoon
and stones to trick an ungenerous host;
stones that rattle the pan at a rolling boil,
to scoop up, blow on, angling the steam
like a god; to be held in the mouth,
hard on the tongue, solid as words.

ii *Scissors:*

I have my own blades to grind:
when they fall I let them lie a while
then warm them next to my heart
before I work them keen again
on the steady, turning stone.

iii *Paper:*

I've made it into boats, tigers,
fortune-pinchers, castles, turreted
and crisp with folding. I've burst
the quiet with it to anger gods, to eke
the long days into longer nights.
I've papered the walls of my house,
its slopes and angles, with the words
of strangers, lovers' messages, with signs.

Alison Brackenbury

Flood

We are made of water. But we forgot.
For twelve long hours the sky sank down like lead
Without a breath of wind. Rain's rush swept slates.
Offices dripped; you broke for home, instead
Of cycling, seemed to swim. Drains gaped like graves
Iron lids askew. Cars breasted tidal waves,

One road, brown flood, one, water spouts. Yet this
Was the storm's lull. Huddled in café's steam
"I've never seen such floods in thirty years"
Travellers gulped down all hopes of reaching home.
As the winds rose, to dry phones' sweet sea bells
They left for schoolfriends, cousins, hot hotels.

Then came the panic. For the pumps were drowned.
In wastes of water, taps would soon run dry.
Then people fought in queues across the town
As bottled water, glittering, swept by
On rain-soaked pallets, for the rain was sharp
As ice. Cars loaded. Then the shops fell dark.

Your gleaming tap coughed empty to the sink.
Surge reached the Abbey, kissed the dead in graves.
You sat by a few pints you dared not drink.
You wished, like your deep fathers, you had saved.
Yet the Ark held. Washed empty by your day
You let the dark's flood carry you away.

Mitchell

Yes, I can see him. He is just nineteen,
As we were nineteen. Ducking out the bar,

Bravo, he lights a cigarette. The gleam
Warms his untouched cheeks, as to a mother,

The tender hollows of his collarbone.
Floods murmur everywhere. He tells the others

He knows the field paths, he is walking home.
What do they hear in dark? A branch's crack,

A child's cry. *I don't know how to swim.*
They have no lights, no rope to haul on slack,

The hidden stream pulls stronger than a horse.
Dark sweeps him on. Day cannot bring him back.

Ten miles downstream, I hack at storm's stunned flowers,
Brush down one whole but thin-stemmed rose, toss it

Into a pail, so I may lose no hours
Of its small breaths, honey and apricot.

Buoyed on the loose soft rainwater, it swirls.
Radio's tides wash over my calm bucket.

A body found in Tewkesbury in fields
Has not yet been identified. But far

In Stroud, in Slad, in Gloucester's cloud, young girls,
The old men name you, see you as you are

Never again. Rose ash falls from your fingers,
The wet door clicks. You walk into the bar.

Bowsers

Boozer writes Confused of Gloucester.
Dazed by screens, I mutter *Browser*—
No. They are bowsers. When I first
Glimpsed one squat blue tank, I reversed,
Leaned over it, not to ease thirst,
But to admire its taps' brass shimmer,
Hissed and spun, its water's glitter.

For two days it stood mainly dry.
On most trips, rattling bottles by
To shops, hill springs, I leant in vain.
Young women walked as to a shrine
Swung buckets slowly, stood in line.
Grandmother's grandfather, I know
Could poise two buckets on his yoke.
Not spill one drop—and light his pipe.

Three ageless women camped on chairs,
Guarded their tank. *You're not from here,*
You can't have this. Then water flowed,
The North-West's tankers blocked our road,
Throbbed bedroom panes the yellow moon rode.
We touched the taps. Cool gushed beneath
Quick as love's spasms, dear as breath.

I spot them now with gaiety.
A white one, look, from Scotland! 'Dee'—
Soldiers hand bottles to hug home.
We need not run when tankers come.
Yet I fear, as the waters hiss,
I need not tell grandchildren this.
They will know what a bowser is.

Litres

You can brush your teeth in one gulp of water
From a clean bottle. You can wash your hair

In one rich litre, catch it in a bowl;
Rinse out two blouses, let the good suds flow

Into the hungry cistern. Haul the tank
Out of the workshop, rig a water bank

Where rain sweeps the shed roof, though you must go
Two hours in storms, to bale the overflow.

You can drive to the farm, where limestone's cool
Pumps private pipelines. With your bottles full

They laugh to see you scramble through the moss
To wrench the tap, so not one drop is lost.

You see Range Rovers where the camp-gear gleams,
Then council tenants, scrambling to their streams.

Your kitchen creeps to boil, you cannot think,
Back aches, clouds sink to heaven. You can drink.

Switched on

After eight days, the taps gush out.
Unwashed, I find the small shops packed,
Children with sweets and squeals.
Each head is soaked, sleeked black,
I bob amongst a colony of seals.

Review

We were not flooded. On our routes
Land stinks of carpet, rotten fruit,
Ashchurch, Tewkesbury.

Tide stopped two inches from our power,
The petrol pumps, the shops' rich bower,
Painswick, Coberley.

Cholera swam in that brown tide.
Yet people lived, unharmed, beside,
Twyning, Ledbury.

We were an island, heard elsewhere
Farm water pump, full washers purr,
Newent, St Briavel.

Now, though the water fades by night,
Though cracked mains spill, it will come right
In Gloucester, Quedgeley, Tuffley.

I cry like water. Do not hope.
Switch off, then walk. Refuse to cope
In Hatherley, Hawling, Whaddon.

The rivers rise, the doomed pumps hum,
The walls are down, the waters come
To Munich, Paris, London.

Anne Cluysenaar

Migrations

Late-night London. The Tube.

Late-night London. The Tube.
Bright lights. Few travelers. I've read
all the poems in the roof. Far to go.
Tunnels and stations. And tunnels.

Doors again. Open and shut.

Then into me, sudden, a voice
pouring that stranger's language,
flesh to flesh! The woman
passes me by, seeking money
further along, comes back
still singing though empty-handed.

As if singing just for herself
the songs of another country.

I'll sit by the red valerian
Hummingbird hawkmoth

I'll sit by the red valerian
with my cup of tea. Early evening.

If it comes at all, it will come
punctually, having remembered
this place in summer's geography.

Ah, look! And it's brought another.

They punch the florets. I lean
to the hum of invisible wings.

Inches only between us.

What do their nerve-cells recall
of the waves biting up, salty?

That inkling they must have had
of all this – somewhere else – existing.

To me, safe on deck, those ships

Goodwin sands

To me, safe on deck, those ships
seemed to have come from beneath,
from a sea under the sea.

Masts piercing the surface
between different dimensions.

Unknown to me, broken-backed ships,
S.O.S. fires – on sands
made firm by retreating tides
then, as ocean floods back,
fatally quick underfoot.

I supposed world within world
prizing matter apart.

Now, I see helpless men
forewarned by the fate of others
feeling the bank give way.
No ground for last words.

Bruxelles. Footings of sand.

i.m. John Cluysenaar , 1899-1986

Bruxelles. Footings of sand.
In his fingers, a shark's tooth.

While he crouches on broken rock,
time surges over. Like seas.
Vibrations. A taste of blood.
Lost world, sunk in cross-bedding.

His own box of bones, the skull
he looks out from, at once flung open
to forces stretching beyond.

Now his work windows my walls.

Making heads of a changing world.
Making world of the human head.

Edges of canvas no more
than where lines reach in, reach out.

I watch her fingers meditate

I watch her fingers meditate
as she puts them aside.
A gesture I never saw.

Did she guess I might keep them,
my two white toddler-sandals,
into old age? I am older now
than she ever became.

Doing my rounds in the barn –
fantails, feral cat, horses –
they've caught my eye once again
in a jumble of things I can't use
but won't chuck away.

As if I could feel a weight
in those tiny feet, my feet –
carrying them to the house –
are feeling themselves responsible
for where we go next.

Her eyes are green, with ochre

Her eyes are green, with ochre
round the centre – that blackness
through which I am looking at her
and she at me. As once,

bicycling an empty street
at night, I looked down on myself.
Terror of being just there –
knees, body straining, two fists –
then of not getting back inside.

Sometimes alternative words
are like that. Are like this. My hand
trying what I tell it to try.
'I's receding through she after she.

A metaphor for this earth
Tintern Abbey grisaille

A metaphor for this earth.
Stone transfixed by light.
Letting in green reflections
and the winging shadows.

They gave up the story of Christ
for translucent tracery.

And the stonemasons' skill
preserved, in slim strong mullions,
an orderliness of change,
layer on layer of sediment.

So that now, in this ruin, looking up
from our own thin soil
to empty unbroken arches,
what Cistercians honoured we see –
woods that teach better than books,
the light growth needs.

But suffer the silence too.
Our hum of admiring chatter
taking the place of praise.

It began with a rabbit bending
for Bonnie Thurston

It began with a rabbit bending
her ears down, to wash them,
on a misty November morning.

While you described her to me
I imagined you stepping closer,
as if you were both in Eden,
neither frightening nor frightened.

It seemed courteous to speak, so you did.
Her answer? To turn a head
with startling signs of survival –
pink skin for eyes, healed over.

So here we were, two humans,
theologian, poet, discussing
a rabbit who certainly lives
with reduced options. But lives.

Ever since, I find myself touched
by three rabbits. A rabbit
greeting the dawn. A rabbit
who must have developed her senses.
A rabbit, for us, metaphorical.

Mere canvas - flat, timeless

'We live in a rainbow of chaos' – Paul Cezanne

Mere canvas – flat, timeless.

Contradictions of light betray
hours when he waits between touches.
Pine-needles blurred by nearness
reveal an ache of distance,
bring closer the bulging rockface.

Through his eyes, Mont St.Victoire
thinking itself. And him.

For me, it's the tensions – air
full of that moving light
from far beyond earth.

Thistledown, dragonflies, cloud.

Shapes vibrating between.

Nothing still. Nothing alone.
Co-presences.

Defying syntax.

No, I can't remember his words

No, I can't remember his words,
just the impression left me:
of a young man hurtling zig-zag
through the rush of air, with snow
spurting from under his skis.

A sense of home life awaits him.
Unguessed, is the war ahead.
His escape, on foot, across borders.

Whenever the snows lie deep
on our Welsh hillside – yes, less
and less often, now – I remember
his memories of snow, passed on
in the language I'm using here
but neither of us were born to.

The track of a fox veers
under wire, trailing spots of blood.
But I won't blot out from my mind
that fenceless mountain: it shimmers
above our snows, while his voice
has survived both words and himself.

Meaning to understand you

Meaning to understand you
I turned from the mantelpiece,
as you had, and spoke aloud
those words you spoke when you left.

I knew you were gone – your footsteps
were still on the stair – but the stance,
the taste, all at once they were with me,
in me, your breath was my own.

I'd invited your heart, left behind,
no matter your words, to draw me
after you – so many years –
and after your death to bring you
back, to warn me in dreams,
again, how painful it would be.

Fossil of its amber forest

Faint as a finger-print,
the seed in its heart would never grow.

But for me the message was rather
how destiny may be folded
on just one particular day
into something, by chance, lasting.

After years at my throat, the drop
broke in two. Amber's memory
had caused the weakness: each half
held a perfect ghostly print.
Where the seed touched both.

They set a great oak upside down
2049 BC

They set a great oak upside down,
as if to grow out of air
into earth. Imagined a future
prepared in the under-world.

They circled to celebrate spring,
summer and autumn, but winter
most of all, when deep out of sight
acorns would come to be shed,
forests begin to unfurl.

In times grimmer than ours.
they dared such a metaphor.

As for me, when the ghost of our oak
hangs in these shallows, unfurling
as if into depths of bright air,
I re-focus my gaze, on mud,
stones, knotted roots
strained by the tree's live weight,
washed bare in the current.

But still, illusions of foliage
silver its flow. Ancestral hopes
reach toward mine. That matter
go on becoming. And becoming thought.

Andrew Bailey

Honeymoon Sketchbook

failing to fall
asleep my wife's
right thigh in
  my new
  left hand

*

you look for the chin while shaving
or later checking—no surprise—
but when you lean to neaten up
a tie's dimple this clean face leaps out;
so this thin ring, so—cutesy,
but what better excuse—so love.

*

confetti forbidden, but later
inordinate butterflies

*

ba-fucking-lloons!
  and laughter
    something spectacular

*

diagonal in driveway
fallen champagne cork

*

a bat last night
emptying the space
  by the house
of its insects swoops
so close it startles
  not so close
as to drive her away
from the seeing of it
there is a transfinite

24

number of things I enjoy
less than eating sushi
on a train with you

*

wind farm at fleetwood
far enough to seem
nigh on imaginary
pale against pale
and still beautiful
as is wife

*

there has not yet been a day without rain;
this past half-hour has been a space without sky,

and rainfall reaches us heavy, white noise
over the flagstones deepening, becoming

instants of darning mushrooms, upsplashes
handles, a glaze across the paving, deeper

but behind the absence of sky was cloud,
white cloud, as nothing detaches, passes

gives way to horizon, to texture,
to even the blue between

*

—shall I fetch a glass of water?
—you just need to lie there,
she said, beam out love,
that's all I need

*

and now
I can run to seed
I mean to fat

Rebecca Gethin

Bestiary

The eye with which I see God is the same eye with which God sees me

Meister Eckhart

I

A low mist skulks where land frays into bog,
sedge, sphagnum. My boot unsucks

and the vibration of my footfall
snaps open a springe, a tautness whirrs

as the sheen of wet earth tears itself from the ground,
fans open into arrowed wings

mottled by peat and cloud-reflecting water,
unleashes itself into air, marsh light dazzling free

and something of myself I hadn't recognised till now
hurtles away, calling out in my own voice.

II

Nesting inside my clothes.
they fly in and out of my pockets,
wing-beats thrumming inside my ears.

They flicker into the sky
still attached to me
by invisible elastic threads,

down which their clock-work
voices vibrate into my sternum
as if I were a lark chick hearing

what I must become – a pouring out
of song, luring danger away from
what I hold most dear.

III
Mist spills out of a gap between hills,
jostles like a pack nosing out quarry
on the run among forest trees.

It haunts the oxbow river, before rising
toward me, as if catching my scent
from where I'm stood on the top of the hill.

On the leading edge of the squall
a sickled form, the colour of slate
and sharp as a talon,

carves itself out of the silvery gust,
rides the crest of the weather front—
hooked beak, wedged tail.

Stretching the curve of her wings
she tilts to one side, vanishes
over the brow as hail stones sprinkle,

then cling to my hair, bounce on the ground
like poems I can't hold for long
in the warmth of my palm.

IV

Like a procession of lit tapers
they cradle themselves across the deepening
water. Poised on their own reflections

necks bend to kiss their own shadows,
rippling like fish at the touch point.
Birds of snow that can't melt—

they dibble their fill of stream water
tipping back their heads to trickle it down.
The falling tide shepherds them out

to where it's undrinkable—
as though thirty candles floated, each one
shielding the small flame of their beaks.

V

Summer rain has fattened the river,
the waters alert, dark as a holt.

Down the race currents gather,
jostling each other to merge

in the pool below. Under-tensions
wrinkle the surface. A ripple firms

into a jink of fur, undulates
into a clay-coloured pelt.

Purpose flows from whiskers
to the tip of a straight-ruddered tail

as he rides the undertow, steers through
the backwash, burrows into the depths.

If you wait and watch for his return
you'll hear the river's many voices utter his name.

Will Kemp

Welcome to Holland

The Amstelkerk tinkles above
lime trees by the Prinsengracht,
grey-green water slaps against
its thin brick sides roped to
cannabis-growing houseboats.
The fluted hoot of a tram ticks off
some bicycles clinking over
a hump-back bridge; a huisvrouw
pleads as a pulley hook hauls
a piano up to the bell of a gable.
The foreman shrugs his arms,
then frowns as she leaves.

*

Down the Herengracht,
the captain of a rondvaart points
to the seven bridges, tells the same stories –
Pieter and the Dyke, the Weepers' Tower –
seven times a day, every day,
in perfect German, French and English.

*

At the Spui,
Evelijne hops onto the back of Ghys' bike,
as he sits back, pushing on towards Singel;
she's fine riding this side-saddle style
as long as the cobbles aren't unkind.

In the Rijksmuseum,
the tall figure of Meneer de Wett adjusts
his dark blue blazer then gestures
towards Phil Woods III, standing
before the Night Watch
while listening to his i-Pod.
Phil switches it off, to hear
the old man's words:
This is not appreciated here.

*

In the Beurs, de Hoorn sits back
by his screen, laughing over the phone.

If you think I'll buy stock for that,
then you must think I am a fool!

*

Oudezids Voorburgwal:
Dex adjusts his dreadlocks in the reflection
from a shop window, then smiles
at the way the sun slants
through trees, giving a Victory-V sign
to some tourists as if it was still the sixties.

*

Outside the Oude Kerk,
Marielle sits in a doorway,
hollow-eyed, running fingers
through her straggled hair,
then breaks down crying:
I've no money. Please help me.
All I need is one more hit.

*

Along Zeedijk, Kev steps
in Gary's sick. John pisses at a wall,
and misses. Laughs all round:
how the fuck will we find
the red light district like this?
Burger King, an Irish bar;
Sex and Hash Museums,
the Heineken Brewery tour.
The beers started at ten,
and now it's only four.
John swears he had
a Dutch girl for thirty quid.
Olga. Liked the shaven head.
Of course she wanted more.
Kev kisses three lions on his shirt.
Come on, you fucking krauts, he shouts
in the only language that he knows.

Bonnie Thurston

The Anchorite

Explains Solitude

Living alone
is not a luxury,
but Babylon's furnace,
fierce, refining,
uncushioned.
Unlike Daniel's
three young men,
I come singed,
smelling of smoke.
It is the price
of walking
with the Fourth.

Offers a Disclaimer

It is not my job
to hold the universe
together,
to solve the past,
to plan the future,
only to be here,
awake.

Visits a Great Cathedral

We do not live our lives
at the High Altar
but in side chapels
of quietude where
what is really present

goes on out of sight
of the nave's big events,
where candle light flickers
only in peripheral vision.

Rises Early

We must rise early.
How else can we see
the sky full of stars,
but low on the horizon,
as if bending
to kiss earth's darkness,
presage dawn's embrace,
provident daily reminder
we are not forgotten?

Gives Thanks

I thank you
that the day is quiet,
the sun is bright,
that awareness of you
dances in consciousness
like autumn leaves
against the blue sky.
It is a happiness
to need only this much
of your infinite variety,
to love your dying world,
to know love undying.

Praises Birds

It was a cold night.
A sizeable community
of slate coloured juncos,
charcoal gray coats
bobbing over white bellies,
pick in the frosty grass
where carefully kept
crumbs from the bread board
were flung with abandon.
Perhaps only in this
am I like unto God:
I know them worth
infinitely more than
two for a penny.

Awaits Spring

Just when spring
should arrive full of sap,
an Arctic Clipper
rattles through
dropping, once again,
winter's lumpy eiderdown.
Icicles form on gutters,
silvery, arthritic fingers
pointing accusingly
at frozen ground.
Sun on hoar frost
makes everything glisten.
There is a crisp sound
of ice falling from trees,
the drip, drip, drip of winter's
witch fingers melting,
enlivening waiting earth.

Anticipates Easter

When the culture
has gone mad
as a March hare,
the steady sanity
of quiet people
who want to live
alone with God
appears crazy as crocus
poking up through snow,
Lenten purple,
but promising Easter.

Explains Poetry

I do it because
there's nothing else
I can do.
I was made for
long listening,
solitary watching,
the almost inaudible
Word.

Delivers an Imperative

In the midst
of the shouting
and squalor
an exquisite lotus
silently unfolds
petal by
intricate petal.
Attend to it.
This whole
remarkable world
is on fire.

Derek Sellen

A Guide to the Spanish Painters

El Caballero De La Mano En El Pecho
on the painting by El Greco

Six bright co-ordinates pick a shape out of the darkness:
the face, the ruff, the lace, the hand, the hilt, some braid.
Later you see the slope of cloaked shoulders, one dropped,
as your eyes conjure the whole man, El Greco's mournful
caballero.

The hand is splayed across the chest. Two conjoined fingers.
A deformity, a secret sign for Jew or Jesuit, an act of will?
Does a damp webbing bind their inner lengths, a frill
of amphibian flesh like the one that fuses a mermaid's legs?

Either he is your hallucination or you are his. Involuntary,
your own hand practises the sign. The caballero looks the kind
who sleeps one hour out of twenty-four, eats sparsely,
shuns women, aches in the night for what he abstains from.
    Your eyes lock—the one to hold the gaze is the one who wins.
    His knuckles shine. When your breath stops, his begins.

An Urchin Searching for a Flea
after the painting by Murillo

What should we have done with the boy?
                    He'd secreted himself
out of the harsh sun, in an alcove of shadow,
l'enfant sauvage, hunting a flea with a cat's intent.
We looked in the window of the old summerhouse
and saw his focused face. He palmed the bug
and slipped it in his mouth, caught sight of us and growled.
His skin was raw with bites and scars, his scalp with lice;
we dressed him in our dead son's clothes and let him stay.

Unseen by neighbours, he roamed the walled garden
or hid in the corners, our nameless, unofficial child.
The boy never smiled, never thanked. No hugs, no kisses.
He stoned the birds and rushed us when we scolded,
biting and clawing. He skulked, he stole, and then he left.
That was when our tears broke, when we tended to our own

                                                                    sores.

Preparations

after the cubist still life 'Violin and Checkerboard' by Juan Gris

I circle the violin,
angling it right and left in my mind,
assigning colour to neck and scroll.

I tilt, truncate, the checkerboard,
see edge and face together,
intercalate the black and amber of the floor.

I find stuff with folds and shadows
that offsets grained and varnished wood.

Spaces will bend under pressure
                          as objects bed in,
a sepia score play music to the eye.

I mark the ground,
like the moments of calculation
before the first handprints at Altamira.

Guernica

on the mural by Picasso

*when Colin Powell visited the UN to seek approval for the Iraq war, a
reproduction of Guernica in the UN building was covered with a blue veil to
avoid any jarring images*

1937. What twenty-eight fascist warplanes did,
strafing the ones that ran, bombing the ones who hid,
is imaged in the bull, the horse, the woman and the child,
the spiky light, the discontinuous arm, the broken sword.
It speaks for London in the blitz, Dresden razed by fire,
My Lai, Fallujah, the office-workers in the falling towers…
It burns through any veil, it distorts with horror:
the twisted face of art looks at the twisted heart of war.

One Liked to Sleep on The Left Side of the Bed and One…

after the painting 'dos mujeres en la playa' by Maruja Mallo

on the right. One muffled herself like a Berber-bride
and one loved to drink the light through her skin. One
unnerved you with her silences, one with her confidences.
I was the lover of both; one would lie gleaming
on top of me like a lion at its prey and the other lifted
no more than a hem in the night to let me in. Twins
without even the difference of a mole—who could swear
which was the sphinx in the darkness and which was running
                                                            bare?

Whatever games they played, slipping in and out
of each other's identity, ended with the boating accident,
a mile off the beach. Strong currents, black rocks,
stripped and battered the one corpse that came to shore,
so that I called both their names, cradling her head.
The sea did not distinguish. Like them, it revealed and hid.

La Tertulia
on the painting by Angeles Santos

A room with four women, an inner privacy,
brewing a mood like inmates of a fever ward,
wordlessly synchronised. Light illuminates
a cheek, shadows an eye, accents a brow.
A bold man would anger, a Prufrock would flee,
rather than bear their favourless scrutiny.
Skirts taut across thighs, a bare arm, a cigarette.
It's 1928 in patriarchal Spain. This is a mutiny.

The painting has dovetailed them; under the chin
of the one who observes her own thoughts,
another reads lying on her back. One is upright
on a chair and one reclining completes the square.
Lezzies or bitches, witches or ball-breakers,
they outface the name-callers with the power they share.

La Marquesa
two responses to the painting by Angeles Santos

I
The marquesa looks irritable, troubled.
The room closes in on her, its walls narrowing.

She's annoyed that she has to pose so long,
that the light shows the lines at the sides of her mouth.

The furniture is wrong for this place,
it's what she's saved from a grander existence.

Couldn't the painter have perked her breasts a little,
couldn't she have faked the years of her age?

The strap of her top flops down her arm,
it's almost ignoble how much of her chest is bare.

She may always be irritated when she thinks of this picture
hanging beyond her power to erase it somewhere.

No pearls, no furs, no jewels; but something more beautiful
than these, Marquesa, because you wear them—your silver shoes.

II

Paint what I am. Not one of those flatteries
skimping the truth, where thirty-seven appears
like twenty. Show me with those extra years
of riper flesh, brooding on missed lecheries.
Not in a palace either, but a plain, clear space,
no drapes, no gilding. And as for smiles, I'll
be as discontented as I please. Paint me while
I glower, paint me volcanic, paint my dark face.

You're talented, they'll admit. But female.
One of the puffed-up men in Paris advises
a softer style than in your immature canvases.
I'm not the image for a collector's home. I see it all—
you'll nod and change your palette.
                        But never over-paint this.
This is what I am. I am your 'masterpiece'.

Dream Caused by the Flight of a Bee around a Pomegranate a Second Before Awakening
on the painting by Salvador Dali

The madmen I have known (a few) have been
of the ordinary kind. Paranoid or obsessive,
none of their imaginations has been so excessive
that they could have conjured this: on legs like spun
extruded sugar, an elephant totters under an obelisk,
tiger leaps from tiger from a fish's jaws from a pomegranate.
In two seconds from now, the circling bee will have done it—
stung the naked sleeping woman, who is at double risk

from insect and rifle-tip bayonet. A lunatic over-world,
created out of paint and self-promoting flimflam,
of Salvador the showman, Dali the magus.
You've seen the act before, the moustache twirled,
the eyes goggling hypnotically, and yet...
                        What a dream to wake from,
your flesh still warmed by the breath of tigers.

It was the kind of hotel...
after Bleu II by Joan Miro

where a pianola played in the lobby.
Miro was the invisible pianist
although the tunes that issued were not his.

The liftboy, chin deep in his collar,
was Miro also in disguise
and he eavesdropped on our conversations
and noted down the floor we exited—mine, not yours.

Miro prepared our breakfast, hidden
behind a fogged partition in the kitchen—but no
mistaking the placement of the croissant in the basket
or the artistry with which the butter was displayed.
It was in the gallery

that he finally revealed himself—the depths of blue
which dumbed us and remain longer than our small affair.

Antoni Tapies

The grit of the world is in my lungs; each day
that I incise my presence on the earth,
its dusts accumulate. Ochre, marble, clay,
atoms of all haunt and inhabit me since my birth.

Fabula
after the painting by El Greco

Night—is horror, with figures beyond the fence
shuffling and cursing like blind men in a dance.
The days are conducted under massy clouds
of wind-swirled dust, stinging your eyes.
                              They call you *Fool*
despite the gesture of solidarity—refusing
your seat on the last ship to leave. Perhaps you are.
Even your books no longer describe a world you recognise,
so you heap and burn them, until words are ashes.

A boy stands at the gate, a monkey riding on his hip.
In his pockets, he has his treasures—shells, seeds,
some candle-stumps and bits of wire to tease the wicks.
Long after the heat has gone out of the fire, in the yard
you and the small ape watch, your faces bright,
as the boy blows on the embers and makes the miracle—light.

Daphne Gloag

Black Hole and Ring Of Light

We Knew About Black Holes

Of course we knew of black holes,
overwhelming gravity, the swallowing
of gas and stars: knew that nothing
escapes, not even light.
We knew too of the edge
of black holes, the 'event horizon',
where things look red, are stretched
like spaghetti, the point of no return.
And we knew that at the centre
time ends.

I thought we would not come to the end
of time. But in hospital you said at last
*I've had enough... enough...*A word
dropping like rock down a mountainside.
We could not go on forever, circling
just far enough from that point of no return.

Event Horizon

We thought we knew
about horizons. As we sat
in that Italian beachside café
our eyes were pulled by the far edge
of the sea: we were filled
by distances, the line between blue and blue
always receding. Nothing beyond.

And we loved events, they made for us
a world. The day we flew in Concorde
our blood danced. We passed
the speed of sound high above
the curving earth; day, sky were stretched,

we kept pace with the sunset. Speed, horizon,
and the race with light filled us.
Some days seemed to lack events, but words
flowed between us...words made events
like the changing of leaves on our birch tree
in autumn, brilliant and sombre.

But there are no events beyond
the event horizon.

Time Stands Still

O day if I waste but a wavelet of thee! you wrote
on your new year card—we used to say
this line of Browning to each other. *We will not,*
you said, *waste a wavelet of the coming year*.

Your words were birds on the waves
that came to me always.
Time held us in its flow;
we did not know that outside black holes

time stands still. It would have frightened us,
just as we would have feared
at the edge of the sea a wave
standing tall before us, its glassy curve

of water never changing. Yet on that card
a time that's motionless now embeds
your words like ancient dragonflies
caught in the clarity of amber.

Parcels of Space and Time

Black holes are parcels of space and time, which are never filled, with distorted space outside them

You had much to say on the sculptures
of Henry Moore: monumental stone,
empty spaces...

stone and its absence, and beyond
the absence of stone those variations of sky
and greenness.

We knew about space that was never filled:
There is always, you said,
so much to say.

Of course our space was distorted -
all those books and papers, floor space
scarce. A slight knock, a cascade

of books, no room to move. But our words
took up little room. They lit up worlds.
Words, light moved in circles round us.

But how would you speak
of those parcels of pure space
and time? Emptiness, nothing.

It doesn't make sense, I hear you say.
And now I can't believe in them,
not when I see that photograph:

behind you an Italian lake, a hillside,
a pen as always in your hand. Words
crowd your table always.

their shadows fall from them.
Meanings, urgencies. On the lake
a red boat sails on and on.

Not Only Dark
Some black holes have a ring of x-rays and visible light surrounding them

Nothing but dark, I said
as I drew our curtains on the darkness
of the birch tree and the robin singing
a snatch of late song,

and yet light all round.
And you understanding. The paradox
of light and dark, a black hole
and a ring of light,

in the space between teacups at ease
on the table and pyracantha
scratching the window beyond
as the wind blew.

Now on a small hill, that place
of wind and silence, the silence
of futures... trees
cut off distances.

Stones, gravestones are master there.
But arriving home I take up that book
of Chinese art, your inscription *A trillion
kisses forever*.

I turn the pages, find the vase with peaches
showing flowers and fruit together,
as in that paradise where peach blossom
lasted for ever.

Irrelevant paradise? But I read
again your inscription: *Perhaps this
is a kind of heaven, the warmth of feeling
and memory,*

light circling a possessed absence.

Pete Marshall

Bro: A Snowdonia Sequence

diamond cut
pink Penderyn sky

slow helix of grey smoke

Siop Y Foel cupped
in the hand of the hill;

between gaps
in the herringboned wall

a stiletto wind
stabs the silver cob's flank;

stark black
against feathered pine

gabled walls, lintelled windows,

empty spaces;

at the Welsh knight's grave
hoar breath plumes

a gauntlet of hazel fingers
grips the frozen land

one purpled metacarpal
points north

and inside

scent of rosewood
and sage

patchouli

in the inglenook

crackle of pine

a little wenlock
thrums

hearthstones
radiate

warmth

oakwood and ash logs
are stacked

by a scuttle of anthracite

and baskets of scavenged
hazel tinder

tombstone waymarker
fog and mist and cloud
[*zero visibility*]
alone and lost

tangible
          echoes
                    muffle

the sound of distant water flowing;

on the Migneint
the Tylwyth Teg play the otherworld shuffle
                turn things upside down
light will-o-the-wisp candles
in the spectral portals of sham cottages

make this spongy bogland path feel safer
            somehow

            familiar
as the smell of an old collie's blanket;

            I'm frightened;

not far away a woman stifles a giggle
            a man coughs

much further out the clatter of iron
shoes on cobblestones

            a horse blows

the creak of a leather harness
            the jangle of a bit
                        the crack of a whip
and the wooden groan of a wagon's slow approach;

next morning when the sun rises
over the snow capped peak of Arennig Fach
to burn the fog from the moor

pooled cauldrons of mist form in the valley;

in the part frozen Conwy lake
a sickle mooned reflection
an inverted horseshoe of Glyder hills;

it's mid-January and still the midges rise
incongruous
against a pristine alpine backdrop;

50

chippy wrappers
crushed fag packets
generic lager cans
disembowelled kebabs
take away cartons
styrofoam cups

skidder of twice trod
anaemic dog shit

in charity shop windows
flyers beckon

learn Welsh
Tai Chi for beginners
African drumming tonight

and on the Spar's wall
hand painted in lurid green
and aerosoled pink

Gwenno is a fat slag
English out
MUFC forever
Bryn Jones sucks cocks
Cymru nid ar werth

leaving the village
a glance in the rear view reveals

a local wag's scrawled calligraphy
Croeso
Bethesda
Welcome
[Twinned with Beirut]

the view lies
somewhere
beyond the drizzle

in the stone built shelter

droplets of water condense

on the underside
of the Vaynol slate roof

a cist of granite uprights
set into soft earth

slate black water

almost frozen
slow, viscous,
touched latex

[a neoprene print]

and oiled, mineralish,
rubbed between
thumb and forefinger

droplets of water condense

reluctant
          pendulous
in here
water speaks
echoes itself

an oral tradition
endlessly

repeated

outside
on the old drovers' road

things pass and change

under the lake
the waterfalls
the streams

flowing
sunlight

three boys
small fry

bamboo fishing
for minnows

toes in silt
sunlight on water
flat black stone

skimming
the bridge
the moor

tiers

here and now
there and then

everything
everything

floating away

trail

our

cuts

buzzard

the

wings

fingered

on

spiralling

vale

lazy

a

of

warmth

the

on

high

thermal

stolen

a

of

throat

the

in

caught

the Roman road

a blizzardy wind

under snow
water flows

turf
sod and soil

cobblestoned
sub-strata

antediluvian foundations
layered millennia

out of the white-out

Caer Bach
Maen Y Bardd dolmen
The Dwarfstone Circle
Swan Inn ruin

and at
Bwylch Y Ddeufaen
stones loom
under hissing cables

hum
like transformers;

behind us
footprints follow

outlanders
pass through

settle in
frontiersville
the wild west

townsfolk
mountain men
trappers, hunters,
homesteaders with
violent cabin fever

all out for blood

searching for squaws
and scalps

los indios

tribal affiliations
blood feuds

there are no piazzas
here
no marbled plaza
no early evening
promenade
chic Champs Elysee
tables
bob in the Seiont

hey gringo
you non fron roun here

in this place all stakes
are claimed
this land
is most definitely not
up for grabs

come to hunt the aborigines
eh pilgrim, well
ye'll find 'em right lively

Caernarfon
world heritage site
Dodge fuckin' City
on a Saturday night

after the cut
round bales
      sag
        pregnant
into womby
        earth
        cast
random shadows
        upon
moleskin farmers
        whose
chequerbellies
        bulge
belted and braced
against the gate
of the farm
at their
dealerbooted feet
supine collies
        whimper
while the lurcher

Fizz

twitches, wired
paws the soil
slips the leash
a kinetic blur
          contoured
against the
falling meadow
and in the wetter
          bottomland
fallow bunnies
          bolt

that last walk
we all joked
a little too hard
tried to ignore
the way the pain
in your back
made you bend
into the hill
it was warm
stone walls
sectioned Tal Y Fan
a meadowlark
sang above Caer Bach
in the corner
of the churchyard
the holy well
you laughed
said anything
was worth a try
but we didn't
and now
I wish we had
I wish I'd
bathed your neck
your back

wish I'd held you
softly
in the water
gently
like I did once
when we were young

drizzle immemorial
drew me back to scratch the prodigal itch.
Chingachgook remains,
older now, passive,
chromium mount
tethered to pitting asphalt.

The rasher's smile
still bleeds ketchup,
while cook thumbs ants
on curling Formica;
Elvis lives
in the Tardis,
but croons a different tune.

Birchbark savages ooze
yellow as yolk
onto my plate,
and I can almost hear
the crackle of pine musketry,
smell his old Holborn cardy,
visualize her madness
dancing with the dust;

but the images sting
like slapped legs.

Outside foxgloves wave:
love letters in the sand
warp by the pigbin's peel;
the urinals reek
and seem to bubble burdock;
sacrificial longlegs
dangle hideously
from greying webs.

Our heraldic runes,
carved so many years before,
remain in slate;
porcelain towns,
no mystery now,
brown sadly in china.

Opal Fruits
and ice cream;
I leave the place haunted,
glancing back
like an infant
fleeing from the dark.

equidistant, uniform, lopped;
mottled duckegg bark,
wrought canopy, woven carpet,
almost too much wealth;
a surfeit of goldleaf
and the gaudy light
gleaming uncanny,
iconic,
through an opaque
gauze of mist;
tendrils of ivy climb,

knotted whale eyes blink and
hipposkinned lips on trunks
swallow the arrowed signs;
the path,
leaflittered beechmast,
mud and moss,
trails chainish through
the quarried wood;
in the breeze
each perfectly crafted leaf
falls, tumbles, spirals,
describes
an individual journey home

Nicola Warwick

Done with Mirrors

Formation

Just glass, until the silver back
is attached and it shifts
to something more, shaped by light
and the eye of the perceiver.

Then, the gazing begins,
a magus scrying the obsidian
of an occult tool,
divining the future, the past,
what will or cannot be.

Reflection

The woman in the mirror tells me
I'm looking tired. She frowns,
pouts and shows me lines
I didn't know I had.

In some lights, I look my age,
so I prefer the blur of candle
and dark corners where
I can cache my imperfections.

Doppelgangers—how they met themselves

Two people, who could, under other circumstances,
be lovers, meet, as if for the first time
and shocked by their own faces
recoil, to consider how little
they know of what they feel
and how they view the actual,
as if one sensation could trigger
the distortion of water to artifice,
the clouding of a lens by a cataract.

The properties of glass

What is left, is right,
right is left, sinister
is dominant, dexter defeated.
White refracts into colour, changing
direction, fanning out, a gasp
from sharpening, shattering, splintering,
a shower of glass, a shake
and shudder of facets.

Sleight of hand

I
Give me smoke and mirrors,
a cast of light and projection
of grey, black, silver, the molten
flow of mercury. No light
and it is slate, speechless
as a deep, dark lake
where an object is dropped
and not sent back.

II
Held to my face, my breath
condenses on the surface,
so I wipe away the wet
and reveal the image
of a shrunken hag,
discarded, like the leavings
of a vampire.

Myra Schneider

Kaleidoscope

Discovery

Some days mist wiped out the world that lay
below our house, days grey as the grate heaped
with the fire's ash, thick as the lumpy nastiness
of porridge which syrup couldn't disguise.

Those days weighed on me like art at school:
drawing cylinders, cubes, closed books on sheets
of off-white paper and not being allowed to touch
the boxes of crayons whose colours burned bright.

There was the day I knelt on the nursery lino,
picked up the kaleidoscope, peered into
its dark tube and gasped at the lime-green leafing
circles of purple petals, at the feathery threading

of moon crescents to stars and dots of gold.
One shake and this vision vanished but another
arose and with every shake another. I could erase
and create magical worlds whenever I chose.

Red

is the leaves you try to catch
as they drop into winter, the flare
from the Halloween turnip's heart

to its cut-out eyes, the ducking
for apples floating in water,
the solid prize you bite into.

Red prickles your fingers, spurts
from your knee the day you trip
with bottles of milk on the lid of a drain.

You develop a dread of red
even before it claws you with ache,
leaks from your body and soaks

through pads which you learn
to wrap up and dispose of in silence.
But you can't kill the smell of shame

and you hate red, the cunning
with which it's trapped you for life.
Yet there are days when red

becomes the possibility of wearing
a dress called excitement,
of nameless seeds spreading.

Floating
after Chagall

Standing hand in hand in this room
full of evening—surely it isn't a dream
that we've found one another? The windows
spring open as if aware we can't be held in.

Now we're out there's no keeping our feet
on the ground. Our hearts are overflowing
and look, we're above the street, floating
above the sleeping houses. We're so high

I could touch the moon's tip, stroke
the sky's lavenders and aquamarines.
Slowly they are giving birth to a violet
momentous as our feelings. You fold me

into your arms and I can think of nothing
more romantic than the way we're sailing
towards the massed singing that's emerging
from flowers in a forest of leaf and fern.

Oh look! there's a donkey far below
sitting on the peak of a roof—it's pricked up
its ears and perhaps it's gazing at the blues
of our world. I think it can hear our happiness.

Circling

You can forget the bump into reality
when the colours lost their shine, forget
the blank months, the nothingness of streets,
the bitter grey which ate into your mind.
You have a partner now and a child,
are part of the party game. You all go
round and round, hands linked, revelling
in the movements of legs and arms.
The air reverberates with energy.
The sun comes out, turns your salmon skin
sand-orange. The laughter is amber.

The circling is getting faster—too fast.
Stop! you shout but your voice
is drowned by others bawling slogans.
You're on a roundabout that's out of control,
will be carried away if you don't jump.
The ground's full of cracks and potholes
but bracing yourself, you leap—land
on your knees. You're bruised but it's a relief
to return to the muted every day, to relax
on the quiet paisley of your sofa, switch off
your mind, watch a black and white film.

His Room

On the door: posters, cuttings
and a warning: *Parents Keep Out.*
I knock, am admitted.

He's painted one wall apricot.
The ceiling is striped with rays
from an over-bright sun.

An ominous black dominates
the wall by the window. I'm careful
not to comment on the bicycle tyre

poking out from under the bed
or the waste-heap of books,
boots and unwashed clothing.

*I've got to find out if life
has any meaning*, he informs me.
He is fifteen, I am forty-five

and the meanings I thought I'd found
have vanished. But behind him
I see myself at fifteen overwhelmed

by black and orange, groping
for answers, not being heard.
Heart full, I listen, I sympathize.

Silence

is silver so you try to hoard it
in your small room among books,
folders, boxes topped with dust,
the dangle of computer cables.

The phone rings. You switch it off
but you can't settle to anything—
the walls, the floor and the air
are all infected with a whirr

you can't identify. And the voices
in your head, which are always
on the lookout for a chance
to criticize, refuse to lie down.

What colour is noise? you ask.
There's no reply. You stare
at the screen for inspiration,
at last write: *Tranquillity is gold.*

Panic

I expect it to strike in a scarlet wild
as underskirts swirling in dance,
inflamed as my throat in the grip
of tonsillitis, furious as the bull
that materialized one afternoon
from nowhere in a field where fence
and hedge were far out of reach.

But when sleep refuses
in the pit of night panic is the cur
that never fails to sniff opportunity.
One yap and its bad breath
is under the duvet, its teeth
sink into my neck, it stirs
havoc in my stomach. In seconds

it blows up like a balloon, sucks in
house and mouthfuls of garden, laughs
as an ambulance screeches disaster.
Not red, its apparel at night
but a black which eclipses
streetlight and searchlight, a black
that out-dazzles equatorial sun.

Garden

Day has washed away the dark—road signs
and car bonnets are bathed in light. Go into
the garden where dandelions pit themselves
against primroses and white flutters
of pear blossom settle on the unruly lawn—

or take yourself back to your first garden
where you stroked the furry lambs' ears
in the rockery, picked bobbles in the privet
for their sweet clothiness, ran away
from the temper of Mrs. Goldie next door,

ashamed that she'd called you a little devil.
You knew you must have done something wrong
and for five minutes wondered what—hacking
a worm in two or biting into the crimson apple
your friend stole and invited you to taste?

No point now in trying to pinpoint your crime—
even if you managed to make your way back
you know you'd find the gate locked, know
rattling the handle wouldn't bring an angel
to swing it open. No way to re-enter that time.

The Pit

Is it because green is going to peter out
that I find myself in a field of bleached stalks?
I make my way to a river. Its bed is waterless,
covered with mud cracked as ancient skin.

When I walk on, sand blows into my hair. No birds
are singing in the puny trees. A prickly plant
that's determined to survive in this place
of broken stones, cuts sharply into my shin.

I lean over a cistern hewn into rock. It's edged
with shrivelled moss, its emptiness smells
of death. Millennia collapse: this could be the pit
Joseph was thrown into by his jealous brothers.

And although I press my palms against my eyes
I cannot blot it out—that beautiful coat the boy
was given by his father. Its fabric is torn, its purples
and pinks are smeared with dirt, stained with blood.

Travelling

A city of calcified bones
and mouths roaring hunger
disappears when you notice

a minute green spider running
up your arm. You stop moping
on the settee, put on trainers,

pack a rucksack with necessities
and although you're well beyond
middle age, you set off.

After days, or maybe it's weeks
of travel, you come to a house
with Van Gogh-yellow walls

which seem to offer hope.
Inside there are airy panels
of quiet in the waiting room,

tension slips off your shoulders
easily as a coat and you sit patiently
with the others inside themselves.

The doctor writes you a prescription
which turns out to be a diagram
of the route you should take. At last

the heart-stopping moment
of light hovering on water and soon
you reach a lake that's been fed

by the blue above. You remember
your child once asked: *What holds
the sky up so it doesn't fall down?*

The quayside beckons with a list
of excursions, you board a boat
that's about to sail to *The Island*.

The Butterfly House

As the glass door closes behind me
I'm immersed in the green of leafery and fern

and wherever I look butterflies flitter,
their wings wider than my palms, wings

with crimson panels on purple dusk,
dramatic with mosaics in black and white.

In this new dimension I'm smiling
as if I too were winged, almost weightless.

Entranced, I move among the flying flowers.
And I want to stay in this place so far beyond

my first garden, beyond the other Edens
I've concocted, live in this temple devoted

to nurture. But it's closing time. An insect
with sapphire skirts is supping on an orange

laid out by hands, the air is belled with light.
Lightened, I slip back to the other world.

Lee Duggan

Reference Points

blown through garden whispers
sleep rustles contemplation
where entrail tongues speak easy
the oak sprang forming
I was small
after a stretch
still it is as yet
set in figures
twenty ten and counting
down to perspective
make time
out of it   habitually
blue flashes dapple limbs
pumping the moment
the morning
                to start

time lies growing
answers we believe in
age through smiles
and the unknown
raise children in dance
become a strange memory
never where I left me

delirious
    run on
  words
    wax
the moment
  crushed to
     a void
white noise
     ideals
out of touch
  reflections
I think
   never
  felt so

a symphony of shadows
estates and bedsits
    un claimed

     inside
 my walls
I think
  I love
   my mother
mother in me

never listen to voices
introduce an exit
signs exist but don't show
place photos far from living things
harmonise to the letter m

stars spin frantic
catch my fears
as skin slips to smile
not an expression
long for more

set rules bound by bedtimes
and every other weekend
anyone who'll listen
a dream of stories
wrung forward through

church decorum to
red-eyed wisdom
left in notes marked
as reference points
like lies

stand off from
faces I have been
back beyond me

painful to touch
crisp winged
angles of air
forms to be measured
against blue aesthetic
silent precision
out bred shadows
under gull cry
traffic slows
for a moment
it's real

over the bridge
wet tarmac and
swoosh of cars
violates everyday
show me what I am
a bus ride home
a child swears
if I'm bad it's your fault
a flurry of snowflakes big as stories
no one to show
back home
the kettle boils

he thinks I'm your wife
count sails over tea
run to the rain
pierce the moment
it was ok

sitting on the fence
slide sleight of hand
the reek of you
claiming a place

together skip sleepers
wandering town
to taste all over

a new location
in confused tongues

           admit
the flurry
       more to do with
    isolation
time spent past
            tic love tic love tic
      rehearsed
dream chatter
inside cold walls
clumsily spilling
to de define
deep terraces
webbed concern
                  cornered
dust
        what
      was never
                  there

wedding tales
     fairy bells
stripped to
             fan
  plumbum   pop
metallic head
        it
as
        it is
   tastic
acts
        girl
vincere
slur lead
     tongued
half formed
predicted
        t   e x t
con formation

                to   drift
    day to
re   say
          definition

assume to
        ring answers
elude
to   evade
    like I was
              blame

black white motion
              me's
free play recall
                  edit
herenow definition
devour roads home
untouchable
              hours
every turn
        the instant
where LL meets 57
won't make
              mine
how it is
      to be me
to be
        elsewhere

laughter splashes as my children spin
cars fresh through darkness
blanketed I listen
and start

patterns that totter
just   coming
a spider head
empty eyes hair   a neck
now you have colour
definition
        your own

butterfly flowers and concentric circles
                                boxed in boxes turned to faces

swings
two
ahead
        graduated
            absorption
now
happening
mine

multi coloured bunting
Spurs on their way
frills
                            I can't see
skirts stark as blond
the proud red pinch of patent shoes
floats preside a marching band
rumble Seven Sisters

can't remember mine

kiss Old Holburn Whiskey tickle
sticky pockets penny deep
take tea from a flowered saucer
crumbs saved for sparrow specks
the weathered man rode so he span
curly whirl straws spiralled crinkly chips
skin quivered pudding
three to a bed
beneath a tea towelled giant Pope

nothing changed but lists

jasmine clung to infiltrate
graze my tongue on old hurts
sensation more than memory

blackbluebeat
       d
          rip
      l
       ip
  oooo   **o**   pen
factor4
      re
    mit
gulp   the burn
  stagnant
      re pulse
then it's quick
            Lucky Dog on the hook
            key in the cupboard
            jam and oats
            Road Runner crossed twice
screaming silently
      just to say
        I was there and no one said a word

close with
unsaid
between lines I
gaps that
over waking
turning ever I
keep my head
spread ashes
your shade of brown
mirrored skirts
making all that noise
where it wouldn't be

appropriate
never alter
edge on
life
to become   my hesitation

ripping out pages
for all that
      she did
everything mmmmeasured
meandering meaning
staggered over
a smashed face
won't stay
to be lovely
a p p pose this problem
to stutter from flow
throw something reader
as I address myself
realler

     rain a blurry screen between dimensions
revolve or turn about

a steady hand in pencil
accuracy captures shape
whilst a vague notion makes me
to see your eyes not as remembered
between you

the camera the artist
                    I am lost
left with a long time ago
a long time to go

found alternative
to talk around
not my idea
took a phrase and squeezed
hoped you'd notice
promise slick as
breaths that made it
bounce enunciation
to edit your memory
make mine
pitch perfect

too much obstructs getting on
remembering one way to get off

emphatic rhythms chart
lacklustre cords
            connection
a prickly heat
  search bonds made on
bodies mean more
but a song could satisfy everything

kids weather the death of my mother
against the box of a bigger picture
contemplate place
                    to cover ground

        been here in notes

write something friendly
no mention of legs
or living for moments

strip down
line up
notions of together
                this
soulless
hip hop
bum bum   booom

so when you refuse to answer
I question my question
to hold
bigger pictures
where you belong

9-5 and then some
everything admirable

and I suck it
guilt and dissatisfaction
dumdu dum doo

towered upon
      mess
       slap
      knock
     screw
       leave   me on the come
     down

denier and heeled
fizzed dance
dizzy to slurs
slick backed velvet
label stapled
unending clink
another
?   me

NS Thompson

Anthropology

Anno MCMLXVIII

I

An attic shape. Fair bend of ceiling. An armorial A. It points to the beginning, an attic space beside the chimney pots on smokeless rooftops left hanging in the clutter of a post Victorian world.

Points of departure. Points to the beginning. The rows of back streets looking combed. In shape.

The sociology of shape.

II

Your city dreams a new geometry,
Its cast of steel plate towers lost in high
Rise speculative thought: reality

Looking squeezed a little, it disappoints
With blue skies sandwiched in between the joints
Of what an architectural line appoints.

A Georgian church, a span of overpass,
The bus station, a street once lit by gas,
Victorian arcadias under glass

Of pioneering skylights that once read
Refuge Assurance, roofs where pigeons tread
And dive for scatterings of daily bread...

Along the city roads with fire-escapes
Zigzagged by iron crosses keeping shapes
Foursquare and trim, but still reality gapes...

Alarm bells breaking into consciousness
Where gushing lead pipe overflows express
This was a brickwork that could harbour stress.

III

A stark inheritance, the sociology of shape takes you back to economic history, warehouses dwarfed by ferro-concrete, squat factories revealed in close-ups of glass and brickwork, the strata of another age.

A lesson buried in history.

IV

Below the scaffold, pale foreheads lift ceremonially, ordained tones give order, sanctify this rite of death; hands rise from pages, tonsured heads bestow a blessing on bare brows.

Low peasant brows caked in sweat and grime, hempen collar round each open neck. Hands scarred by thorns, brambles, stripes, minds clutching at the roots of earth, counting the cost. The earth now lost.

...et fut fait sans parler ne sans signer, comme ce ne fussent ymaiges eslevez contre ung mur...

So the bourgeois journal said

A line from history. The world made flesh.

The year the barns burned, the world rebelled and the sun cut ribbons over streaming ground, now sticky, wet with blood. The word made flesh. Shadows scored the earth like knife blades. On furrowed ground, the voiceless found expression.

Feet massacred the spoils, smashed majolica flecked with blood set tongues wagging on the butchered heads on poles.

A lesson in history. A shape for the entire world, putting paid to the dark gods. A fierce new fraternity born in the liberality of blood.

89

V

And where were you? Up against it. Up against the wall. Lost inside a skyline up against the concrete blocks.

You looked down time, imperfect on a cobbled road, and heard it speak to you. The brickwork of another age. The lesson of history. *Aux barricades! Les habits noirs!*

Ho ho ho
Ho Chi Minh
Putting paid to the dark

VI

You found the Union. A gathering in a student bar. The sit-in workshop of a seminar. And there you all sat like young Greek gods triangulated in a tympanum, fingers drumming, tongues wagging, minds waging war. Like philosophers, with mantle furred. Blowing hot and cold, man.

Yeah, Freddie Hubbard, man, not Clifford Brown...
You listen to *Parisian Thoroughfare?*
Well, nobody could ever play like Monk,
No one could quite play like Thelonious...
And was he on the barricades?
Tough bodies shouldering epaulettes
On greatcoats, cool fingers drumming a tattoo,
Rolling a cigarette or two, camouflage jacket bang on target
With a well read Marx, a hand salute from Che...

How different from a year before. A blue serge suit and kipper tie. The sounds of Motown. Fashion brogues. How quickly you had grown. Now beads, an almost Phrygian woollen cap and drooping altogether macho Latin-style moustache. The coolest sign for bivouacs in the bar, harangues to the troops, ready for attack. The end to justify the means. In the beginning – for a start – the casual dismantling of humanism.

Yes, you were up on history's stage with flysheets, meetings, *Black Dwarf, Frendz* and *Oz.* And Piotor Kropotkin. Oh yeah, we were ready for the fight, all right, Piotr Alekseyevitch. Fields, factories and workshops. All organised. Ready for the fight, like...

90

...like war paint on a smart bird nestling by the branches, eyes glinting like a gin and tonic's ice. A sodden Tetley's coaster on the bar...

...like strange exotic fruit dropped from branches and cells. The voices of factory and warehouse, brothers ghostly in loudspeakers in a compound of concrete and barbed wire. What were we thinking? What? The casual dismantling of humanism. But where were the songs, the songs of war, the hard ones, the chants, the slogans? Ho ho ho. Where were the signs? What was the language of the tribe? Apollodorus harmonized on billiards, Agathon discoursed upon the art of joints, young Plato sounded wild on the ideal. The ideal what?

So there we were pressed around the Union walls, a great big frieze, curtains chiselled like temple columns, pillars of the academy. With mantle furred.

Anthropology, the proper study of mankind.

VII

The proper study of mankind is
Proper study of a kind
Is kind of study, man
The study of mankind (kind of)
The sociology of shape...
The goal to dismantle humanism.

Quod mundus stabili fide
Concordes variat vices
Ahem
The world said go establish faith
In concord with its various vices.
Ahem

So said — or not — Anicius Manlius Severinus Boethius of the famous Praenestine family of the Anicii to purify the language of the tribe so said (or not) the merdous Poet of the Po in the captive Pound of Italy

91

Kek kek kokkow quek quek who gives a bugger for Boethius?
O tell me who?
Quoth Bird

What binds all things together see
and governs earth and sea and sky
is love sweet love, you see
Don't ask me why

O felix hominum genus
Si vestros animos amor
Quo caelum regitur regat

Rego regis regit
Nego negis negit
Negro negris
Negritude says

Them that's got shall get, them that's not shall lose
So the Bible says and it still is news
Full Marx

The goal was to dismantle humanism.

VIII

  You walked out of the Union Building, feet slushing through the fallen leaflets, stamping on ideas, feeling a cold wind blow through the black spikes of your being. Being what?

IX

Leaflets rained upon the ground, glistening with ideas. Out in the parks, leaves stirred. Hey, stop, what's that sound? A lunatic in the grass. The lunatic with the grass. You felt the cold wind blowing through you as if you were the black skeletal railing, circling nothing. A splendid O.

Alpha and Omega. The attic and the ending for your green, naïve and sentimental heart, sodden with ideas. Them that's got.

Between the gaps in the railings, the empty swirl of leaves, the circulation of your heart, the dry leaves eddying.

X

The rattle of the railings holding you...

Could no one tame you? Teach you? Take you in? Could no one help you down the crowded pavements? But no, you had to travel them alone...

...and like some poet rise beyond the boredom and despair.

How close you felt to history, drinking in the wine of the barricades, moustaches flying, the red flags of revolution glittering in plate glass where the *habits noirs* poured over the blueprint, tea leaves flecking the saucers, cigarettes squashed on the ground.

The theory of the barricades. On cobbled streets. Your heart laid bare by careless revolution. But with someone hungry by the roadside, how could you consider your admission to the Academy?

Peter Barry

Upholland Poems

Thalassa, Thalassa

The Rector's 'bad back' is MS,
but the stone-flagged corridors
are great for his motorised chair -
you can hear it coming
as we wait for the Greek lesson.

The head boy stands, elbow braced,
between door and rostrum.
The Rector hauls himself from the chair,
grabs the elbow,
and pulls himself up to the desk.

Then we are marching
with Xenophon and the Ten Thousand,
m a n y   m a n y   m i l e s   f r o m   t h e
sea.

The Proper of the Time

Choir practice Saturday night in the library -
it's the half hour before supper,
and cold comfort is coming to us all.

Sammy Snape bangs the lectern
with his tuning fork — *that's a* dotted *punctum*
he snapes at us — *start again.*

Sammy flicks back his Johnny Haynes quiff,
shiny black and slicked heavy with Brylcreem,
and starts us again through Credo III in the *Liber.*

I'm not just tone-deaf, I'm tone-dead—
if only Sunday Mass were a *Missa Dicta*
then Father Snape could pack his bags

and zoom off down the drive in his Sunbeam Rapier,
tapping the dashboard to cue the *cantores*
and intoning to perfection the Proper of the Time.

No Gates on the Drive

When we complain about our lot
Father Cummins listens, then says
>   *Well, there are no gates on the drive.*

There used to be—
they took them off in 1940
to make Spitfires.

>   But for us, the gates are still there -
>   iron bars don't make a prison,
>   nor, I suspect, Spitfires.

Spain Again

The library has bound journals from the 30s
with pictures of Popular Front outrages—
stacked corpses, shelled cathedrals, toppled statues.

The Spectre of Communism is stalking Europe.
If they win they'll take over our college
and make it a hotbed of the Red Terror.

The pro-cathedral in the cobbled back-street
on Brownlow Hill will be a cinema
with a diet of news-reels and *Potemkin*.

Talking dialectics, the Comrades will toil uphill
to the red-flagged picture-house.
The Faithful become the lumpen proletariat.

Would even Communists go there, I wonder,
if it weren't for the free buns
from the food factory next-door?

Food first, then social materialism, the cadres say,
even when there isn't any food.
Only the good Generalissimo can save us.

A Lesson on Macbeth

OK, let's say it's dinner time,
and when the server
brings the dish of potatoes
for your table, one person
grabs the lot—
What do you do?

We quickly see the moral crux:
Clock him one, Father,
and grab them back—
So some will side with you,
some with him -
that's civil war.

Talk to him, then, tell him
it's no way to behave.
Right, so you'll try diplomacy—
what if it doesn't work?

We'll *keep* talking,
and clock him one
if he doesn't listen.
So it's gunboat diplomacy—
and if he's got a gunboat too?

We'll say we understand—
he's extra hungry today; he can have
a double serving, just this once.
That's appeasement—
it didn't work with Hitler.

The bell goes for dinner.
We wonder if anyone
might try it on today.
Father Maxwell closes his book,
and says we'll carry on tomorrow—
        and tomorrow, and tomorrow.

The Feast of Saints Cosmas & Damian

Tuesday evenings the Prefect of Discipline
patrols the ref with a clipboard,
tapping his victims on the shoulder.

The barber comes Wednesdays—
early closing in Wigan—
average through-put twenty-odd an hour.

Still, better him than the doddery bishop
who administers First Tonsure
on ordination days.

When the Prefect says I need a shave—
I answer, *No razor, Father*
and I'm told to write home for one.

22nd November 1963

The Rector rings the bell at supper
and says *President Kennedy*
has been assassinated, and is now dead
adding *pray for his soul,*
as if he knows things we don't.

We know about political assassination—
have done *Macbeth* and *JC*—
the next stage is war.
How long does it take a B52
to fly from Utah to Moscow—ten hours?

Before the football-rattle goes
at six tomorrow morning,
before the bed curtain's flicked back
with *Benedicamus Domino,*
we'll be in Purgatory—or worse.

The Martyrology

On the day appointed
they sing the *Martyrology,*
relic of the secret seminaries
of Douai and Valladolid.

The doors are unbolted
between the two refectories,
and we stand at tables
long as the decks of steamers.

Flanked by candle-bearers,
the Cantor raps his wrist
with a tuning-fork
and intones the running line.

Then we endure the litany
of racked bodies and
faithful until death, sung,
for our comfort, in English.

Father Worden Lectures on Rubrics

By an altar bare to the planks
for Holy Week, a man built like a Papal Bull.

Let's think about familiar things,
about signs that lose their meanings:

the priest at Mass crosses the gospel text
with his thumb before he reads it –

Why do we do that? Which always means,
why did we start doing it just when we did?

Ask a simple question, and we'll be here all day, —
mutters Jas Kelly, unravelling sects and schisms.

Tessera

We're two days into our retreat,
and I'm on the bench by Top Lake,
recollecting my purposes on earth,
and thinking retreat thoughts.

The sandstone towers
are dark with yesterday's rain,
a House of Usher brooding
on its image in the tarn.

The world is the breath of God,
  The retreat father tells us,
            He breathes out, and we're here,
              in, and we're gone.

Then a slow blade of wind
moves across the face of the waters,
brushing away the towery city –
and, yes, I think *Sic transit.*

Pedro González Telmo

By a stilled ocean,
a Dominican holds fire
in his bare hands.

I read this story, about a man
on a sailing ship in a book
in the library, and invented the rest:

We're thirty-one days out—
the masts are blue-tipped candles
held to the Southern Cross,

a cone of light burns on every spar,
the waters shiver with organic life,
our living wake curls luminous behind.

Edging along the bowsprit's ratlines
to reef the foam-flecked staysail, I slip,
and hang head-downwards in the steel-bright air—

and till I swung back up,
with muscles not my own,
I see the ocean, in St Telmo's fire,

boiling white beneath me, and above,
the milky ejaculate of God
splashes through the firmament.

Going Home Day

After Mass we file into the ref,
the drive outside noisy with cars;
then tea and fidgeting, till the Prefect
  dismisses the years —
  each class jumps up with a cheer
  and scarpers.

Arms linked, three Divines rush the corridor,
rising in unison to clear a travel trunk,
and fanning out down the steps into the quad.
Someone calls out to them from top dorm,
and waving in triplicate without turning,
they disappear through the archway
and into the wide world.

Ruth Bidgood

Set Free

I

It would have taken too long
to walk round the lake. We turned back
at the bridge near the heronry,
where long beaky shapes sailed the sky.

Better this way—though, given time,
on such a benign day we'd have gone on,
looping the promontory, catching and losing
sun or water through trees, gone right round
to the start, and all those birds there- scores of them,
pressing in to be fed: stolid Brent geese
heavily plashing in shallows,
a greed of ducks eagerly chugging inshore,
outermost a solemnity of swans.

But better like this: a whole domain
only guessed at—glitter and sway, depths clear
or fronded with weed; leaf-scents, old paths;
none of it certain, none of it captive, all set free
to ghost what we kept of the day.

II

He's a long way off. I can't make out
the white creatures advancing
just ahead of his feet. When he gets near,
they translate, strangely, as doves,
six of them, heads thrust forward, jerked back,
gait a smoothed out shuffle.
You look like a shepherd! I call,
and we both start to laugh, because
that's what he was, in the days of work.
The doves take exception to laughter;

flow on to the road, miraculously
escaping two cars and a lorry.
Reaching the safety of grass,
they are suddenly airborne,
spiralling disdainfully above us,
above rooftops and trees, dwindling
between hills, freeing us
from dailiness, lifting us
into a vision of wings.

III

There are places whose nature seems
random, bitty, humorous even,
like this patch, (hardly a field)
I'm passing close in the small train.

It's fenced, each side, with wobbly pales;
behind sprout the back-kitchens
of tenements. I'm surprised
by colour. Certainly the grass,
surviving in flattened lumps,
isn't really green. Yet the litter
is cheerful—squashed plastic buckets
minus handle, shouting red;
rich rust of metallic debris, grass
weaving in and out of struts and rods.

Backing it all, those houses. They've been
colour-washed, once, all different-
blue, pink, yellow, one a kind of
half-hearted purple—and now
are faded, peeling, but still have an echo
of care for the eye's delight.

As the little diesel crawls by
I'm left with a sense of something
damaged, but laughing; something
fragmentary, but adding up
to a livelier identity than you'd find
in sober, tidy streets of the hinterland.

No-one expected much
of this almost-field—
it's free of that burden,
free to be its own
scruffy insouciant self,
free to display its art
of quirky celebration.

IV

I remember a bend
in an unfamiliar road,
patchy colours of a wall,
the angle of a house
by a stunted tree-
all snatching at my mind
as I passed.

There were no links
with my life, no giggling or tears
of long-gone children, no pandemonium
of the heart. Yet something brushed by,
uninvolved in any memory of mine,
free to wake a sudden sense
of the parallel, unpredictable, free
to let me catch from far the tiny clear
bell-song of the unexplained.

V

...the truth shall make you free:
what frees me *is* my truth-
a long lane climbing out of twisted oaks,
above the curling tumble of a stream,
into the hills. Not possible to see
any time, any out-of-time moment,
when I won't be part of this.
I'm shackled by air and grace,
my truth a fettered freedom,
my day eternity.

Susan Richardson

Translations from Maeshowe

Raise your fingers to my face—make me know
the deep, slow thrill of being decoded.
In the glow from your torch, let my skin show
its flaws—rough, yet mostly uneroded
for I've never sought the touch of sea or
storm. Probe all of my notches and niches,
each sword-straight score. Translate me into your
more graceful script with its smoother features.
Urge my rigid grooves to learn to loop, curve
and curl, un-curse me from stone, teach me how
to sprawl across your page, swing my hips, swerve,
like a ship without a solstein. Quick, now—
unhitch my mental belt, ditch my tunic,
don't desist till I quit being runic.

Ofram the son of Sigurd carved these runes

Ofram licked the surface
after carving,
felt the imprint of the chipping
on his tongue.

Before,
he heard the wall's Norn pleas
and the scorn in his father's voice;
the warning.

Ingigerth is the most beautiful of women

i want to listen for the murmur of your skirts Ingigerth as you move between dairy and byre when you stoop to light the fire beneath my cooking pot i want to reach as sure as an oar through water for the harbour of your thighs and then i want to lie with you Ingigerth under wadmal dyed dusk-lilac instead of with nettles and piss and i promise you this Ingigerth i will not curse call on thor tongue my drinking horn till my head hurts like amber i'll not be gruff bluff daytime i'll make a brooch from the moon for the shoulder of your dress i'll add my need to a string of glass beads and let it rest between your breasts and then i'll enter you like the sun illuminates this tomb's entranceway on winter's deepest day and she who gave birth to you Ingigerth should be buried here with fourteen slaughtered horses as a queen i mean every word of what i say Ingigerth yet my hope falls through the hole in your soapstone spindle whorl for you are wedded to Egil and he is not so beautiful

Hlif the earl's cook carved these runes

Hlif is sick of cooking.
Most days, Hlif spits
in the earl's stew.
Hlif carves to prove
he can read
and write too, and in a different age
Hlif would move on
to make runic jewellery.
Hlif would open a bijou gallery
with adjacent studio.
Hlif would be part
of the Art Trail for Tourists.
In summer, they'd shuffle in, puffinly,
through pink thrift and rain.

Many a woman has had to lower herself to come in
here whatever their airs and graces

Their woman airs herself
and many come in—
here come their graces.

Many had a woman in here
and their woman
—their lower woman—
has had many herself.

Their woman graces herself.
To herself.
In herself. Here.

Come. Come lower.
A woman has to.

Whatever.

Tholfir Kolbeinsson carved these runes high up

He's so tall
that Thor's thunder's
inexhaustible
in his ears. Blown
off course,
rare migrants
pause for a while
in his beard. He
plunders the sky
for stars, weaves
sacks and sails
from the strands
of the aurora. On
his head, instead
of a helmet,

he wears a cap
of ice. He singes
his fingers on Bifrost
but could cross it
in three strides. And
each spring, it's he
who decides when
to use a knife
to hack through
the roof of night
to let the light
back in.

Ingibjörg the fair widow

she misses the days
those lazy, post-raid days
when he'd return
with church treasure and jewels
and a new slave

and she misses the nights
when the sky
would turn purple with pleasure

and now she plucks and
cards and
fingers her drop spindle and
tugs udders and
seizes moss and
seaweed and
at times her hand strays
between her parted thighs
till she startles the sheep
with her cries and then

sorrow raids her brain and
loads everything but pain
onto a longboat
that leaves with speed for Norway and

she weaves her grief
on an upright loom
her weeping the warp
her loneliness the weft and

with each in-breath
her breasts strain to raise
the Standing Stones of Stenness

Arnfithr Matr carved these runes with this axe owned
by Gauk Trandilsson in the south land

Squeezed on the sleeping bench,
his limbs are tinder.
If he moves, his shins will rub
and start a fire.

Deep night—
he's a too-ripe fruit.
Juice leaks from each crease of him.

Half-dark—
heat rounds up
the sheep he counts.
They dehydrate and die.

Thin light—
he kicks off
the frayed layer of sleep
to see the crater of his navel steaming, unsure

if he's still dreaming
of a south land
in the north.

Away to the northwest is a great treasure hidden

Away to the northwest
are women who flipper up storms,
whose fingers can't tickle, type
or hold a fork
but who've learnt to talk
dulse and bubbles.

Away to the northwest
auks order their interval fish,
claim the swishest seats,
then sit in stilted rows—
hoping the men with nets on sticks won't show—
with nowhere to go
and nothing to do
but swallow.

Away to the northwest
sheep bleat in their deep green sleep
and the dream of blue
is as frivolous as Icarus

Away to the northwest
a stoned witch bitches
about her wet feet,
while beneath its cowl of fog
a mountain growls
that *F marks the spot*.

These runes were carved by the man most skilled in
runes in the western ocean

He's seen them all—
the one whose stone fort, dizzy
with history, hurls itself
at the fizzing sea.

The one hunched under
a sealskin sky,
its sleek grey curve whiskered
with sun.

The one with just enough grass
for a lone sheep to thrive,
two to survive
or three to starve.

But he's grown tired of trading,
raiding, all the talk
of more orkneying.
As of now, he's stopped
runing and will soon   float
                          boatly   away.

Ruth Thompson

A Love of Weather
poems on places connected with the New Zealand writer, Janet Frame

Silkworms

Wild-seeded sweet corn, a paw-paw tree,
the trespasser treads here softly, listening for
the tapping of her typewriter, half-expecting
a *quick-brown-fox* to lope out of the old army hut
and cross the lawn with a glance to the east wall,
where Frank, naked, takes his morning sunbathe.

In the porch there is bum-worn wooden seat.
Filmy windows frame an armchair, a bookshelf,
and in the corners cobwebs have snared
leaf-filtered sunlight, sticky woven hints of how,
when all there was between them became
too stretched they turned to silkworms.

Together they tended the feeding and growing,
the shifting and shedding, the blaze, the cocoon;
choosing to spin, not reel, the strands of silk
they harvested. When she left he buried the last
batch of eggs in the garden, intending to bring
them back some spring, some dawn. Imagine—

those pale Lazarus globes still shimmering beneath
paspalum. Even now, if there was digging
they might hatch, bringing forth small revelations
of a silvery pulpous sort: delicate, easily damaged.

Numero seis, Calle Ignacier Roquer

Signor Ramon now has his office here,
he opens up the heavy wooden door,
and steps across the red-tiled porch among
the sounds she heard - church bells,
men's voices surging from a bar.

All skirt and jersey (sandals slapping up
the hill past balconies where knickers
aired like cauls) she was returning
from the sea, from floating in a milky-warm
sea-urchin drift, knowing it was time to seek

a room that smelled of snow where she
could roost and brood alone in winceyette
until, a suppliant on a wobbly kitchen chair
stretching up towards the light,
she received blood's dark solution.

Home, criss-crossing Clapham Common,
she carried in her head that reddish jolt:
a broken Spanish tile, a Scarlet Tanager in snow;
arrived too soon, too far off-course.

Walking to the Maudsley

From the door of number 39 (share electric)
past the hostel for the blind on Grove Hill Road
buddleias, self-seeded, weeping

with the weight of purple flower-spikes
(she has a love of weather, sky and sea),
turning right at Dog Kennel Road

along Grove Lane remembering last night's
sleek man with beery breath who called
his kiss *a token*; crossing Champion Park

then right down Denmark Hill, still
unspooling words like thread until, safe
inside an office in the Maudsley she speaks

of how, when evening comes she switches on
the light, turns to draw the faded curtains,
and must face herself, alone.

9 Juliet Street, Stratford

The house she thought would be the last
before the last has been knocked down,
its timbers, painted cornices are gone,
the naked plot raked over; a broken glint
of crockery poking through like bone.
Next door, a pensioner sits knitting and
I wonder if, when holding up a half-
completed jersey to admire its length
and tension, he sees that words have
taken shape among his plains and purls.
A mention of a *goldfinch* or a *gull*,
a phrase in Spanish, *long-lost Figueretas*.

Stray words that, drifting up like motes from
paper flowers were captured in her ceiling
corners, and now released, are knit
together in the seedbed of his stitches.

Wanganui to Levin

At first there was more wheeling than flying,
as she puttered to the dairy
for milk and mail, carrying it home
to Andrew's Place in a wicker basket
fixed to the front mud-guard.

Then, realising that a motorcycle's power
lies in a state of grace,
she braved the tenuous art
of balancing weight with
the heat of contained fire

and set out from Wanganui,
thin skin thickened with woolly layers,
sailing the wind-farts
of passing lorries, staying upright,
wild, euphoric, *breakable*.

At Himatangi someone attending
to their roses looked up to see the flaming arc
of her approach, then stood a while,
as if diminished, in the silence when she'd gone.

Gonville

Streets of small, blank bungalows adorned
with driftwood garden ornaments and
sea-rolled stones: the meat-works, a marae,
a dairy where postcards offer pups and pigeons.

The house at Andrew's Place squats box-like on
a corner: silent, empty, yet in the garden
blooms her tender oleander, and a cat
(although tortoiseshell, not white) licks amber
fur with care beneath the palm.

A small motorbike appears, a rounded woman
balanced in a state of grace—a Gonville angel,
snagged in this one lustrous moment by
a mirrored southern light: prismatic, *passing*.

Tony Curtis

Swish back west:
six poems for the painter Brendan Stuart Burns

1
When the tectonic plates of paint
shift and collide
what, as well as being,
are we put in mind of?

2
> It's misty wet with rain
> and the glasses
> of the world slip
> across each other:
> the smudge of life
> born in a conspiracy of colour.

3
Debussy Preludes:
above the drowned cathedral
float lights that make no sound until
you hear the shimmering
circles of columns,
see the sunken bells.

4
Edging west—
as the day falls away to Ireland,
catch all the moments.
Thumb and knife and brush:
that last spindrift year lost.

5

Liquid light.
   Taste of sight.
      Sky pools.
         Not the stillness.
           No, something about to be.
              In motion.

6

Rock pool constellations
that mirror this world,
and map worlds we cannot see:
craters, rock and pebble, fronds,
the brief movement of life
in embroidered salt and air,
light you can taste.

Sue Rose

Heavy Elements

Lead

Too slight for his clothes, he was filled
with lead the midnight we arrived
to find him half on, half off the bed.

The next morning, flopped forward
on the bedside stool, arms dragging, head
on knees, it took a man's strength

to Heimlich him back—the younger body
a winch, legs rollers, torso a pallet—till both men
lay side by side on the tangled sheets.

Mercury

This death runs like quicksilver
through the blood branching
beneath her skin, withering her

ring by ring. She's sinking
under the pressure, a barometer,
lower than ever before.

Her widow's hump crests
as her body bends like a cane
under the burden of vacant air.

Oxygen

My passenger seat is empty. No more
converters, blocky as valve amps, huffing
their square music into our hall.

No more hospitals, tank shouldered
to navigate the hostile air, cannula pipe
twining round handbrake and gear stick

like the convolvulus he used to rip up
by the handful, face beaded with sweat,
as he unbent to catch his breath.

Carbon

In this urn, his new shape,
his shapelessness—frame, stomach, liver, lungs
returned to their essential elements—

five pounds' weight of variegated gravel:
grey charcoal, yellow unburned trabecular bone,
white ash and black carbon, waiting to join

hers in a hotter furnace, forming diamonds
for their daughters, fashioned from high heat
and pressure, hard enough to last.

Bruce Ackerley

Welsh Roads
from east to west: a road trip into nostalgia

Border Country (The Door)

We'll know the land when we see it,
its dank, undistinguished heaven of fields
with gorse and their bleating young.
The same clouds go on down the same
veldt of sky and a house remains there—
around her the dormant woods, the chequered
gloom of pine and commissioned firs.
The orchard's run to seed; the paths lead nowhere—
just as they should. England's an hour's
drive and a light year away but everything
has changed: Nantyr—as if I could,
or ever will, play the boy to your stream.

Vrynwy

And so I set up a land of the mind.
It was all solace; plotting
the hawthorn's yield, the sheep
flecking the hills like grubs.
And then, there was that other life,
rendered pure by its own fiction.
Fragments from a past I hadn't walked:
dormers and dressers and stars
picked out in upper rooms. Childish
rancour met by a mother's calm;
a farmer's son—hands knowing
the muck in a cow's birth; Red
Kites on a lake's antimony;
a decade of summers bellied in grey
and lost to all but artful regression.

Glynn Ceiriog Spring

It's bright, almost hot.
The Cherry's showcasing
her gaudy pinks.

The latest Easter we have seen—
an open dormer, the wood's
cologne after dusk.

All winter I stored the habit of our days,
a wall against ruin. Just now
I'm light enough, even trivial.

Give me time and I might
even surprise us both:
break the mould and start living.

Glyn Ceiriog Summer

Save for the stubborn Ash,
still dragging its heels,
the woods are a foam of green;
here and there a rarer blue
pockets the sky's grey insufficiency.

How much of the year's gone to waste?
It's June and I've no sentiment for cold:
summer chill being a furl
of cottage smoke, dead-ends
sketched out beside the fire.

Map us both the route—
the one dream nagging
like a child; the old, geographic
fallacy that swings our compass west:
a stubborn arc over field
and rock and col, Snowdonia's
tumbledown, and out across

the Lleyn's far tilt into the sea's
abstraction. A panoply of myth:
tall tales of days long with light
and a house where we never lived,
white-washed behind Neigwl.

Sygun Fawr—June 08

Not a summer to speak of.
Four days counting
the sun's favour
on a single hand.

Palettes of grey;
everywhere
the poured lead
of random streams;

a sort of
Japanese motif
of cloudy hills:
lithograph for *Hiroshige.*

By the path,
cowled firs
breast the slopes
like pilgrim;

rising early,
a lone and tasteful
thunderclap
announces the morning rain.

Washout

Swore we'd never go back.
Wet mutts dragging the trail
of my private longings—
those days in that short-
stay park a life-time
at your disposal.

At the coast a low
and glowering light,
inland the drowned moors;
the Lleyn beading
the gloom with hills
down to Bardsey's
low and monkish seclusion.

Fair play to you,
cutting to the chase:
that sunlit, perfected
beach of youth lives
best where the grass
is always greener:
leave it there.

Maltraeth

Beyond Llandwyn
the summer crowd
thins to a trickle.
In light or cloud,
with, without
the shriek of youth
Maltraeth's a cold fish.

Something in the gaunt,
autumnal coast,
the spooked house
in its horseshoe of trees
that feels so…
irredeemably northern.

One thinks
of another beach
down on her share of sun:
a tight-lipped cousin—
blonde and empty,
lovelorn Scarista.

Newborough Church

From Caernarfon's shore
the trained eye
might pick her out,
a broody silhouette;
her plain speech
recalled more often
than she'll ever know.

Stands head-on to the wet;
a little dour but still
a whiff of the Celtic.
Generically spiritual—
gatehouse to that other
mistress life of the heart.

Porth Neigwl

No cure for the restive hour you go there often,
a lone gull fitting yourself into darkness.
Riding the slopes of gorse behind Llanengan's fold;
up and across Fadrum's presidential mound;
bleak and soft, as ever the same path over
bald fields to the bay in moon or storm-light,
lately vexed, Autumnal heat. It doesn't matter:
mid-way through a sleepless life these are small acts,
smaller compensations, with the prize
in the going, in bringing home the numb mind.

From Y Rhiw
after Sicily

Turning, you slow the car
and looking back
our latitude pulls south
to another scene:
a sudden chimera
calling to mind
the clemency
of a half-forgotten coast
on the road to Syracuse.

Impostures
of Mediterranean light,
phased blue the hour
will fast negate —
the storm's
prevailing truth
on this maw of wind:
blackened and roiling
belligerent Neigwl,
the mind's due-North.

Porthceiriog

My mother is warming to her theme.
Broadly speaking a fifties summer.
A house and a beach, her brother—
her mother? possibly, she can't recall.

On the face of it, sobriety, or at least
a steady joy and at today's rate priceless.
Running water at a push; gas lamps
after hours: a farmer's track melding

through dunes to a shore and a place
where recollection kits out the past
with a shrine: surfeitures of light
in the rose of nostalgia.

Llanbedrog Head

Looks like I'm doing it again—
freighting these views
with meaning, travelling
once more addicted
to a managed past,
as though every journey west
were a decades-long reversal.

Tumbled giant you rest
in the calms of the bay
and I revisit the week I came here—
a boy on the fringe of greatness;
unsexed; all future roles
deemed possible; guessing
little, then, how much
of the page lay printed.

Wendy Klein

New Orleans

Lagniappe
after Eudora Welty

She lands on a wedding cake,
where the wings of the plane flap,
fold, shudder with tenderness;
melt from the heat of a thousand

candles. She threads a path
through carnival where beauty
and vice stand, hospitably close—
fan themselves in doorways

under palmettos by day, lighted torches
by night. A flower opens. She feels
the pull of the bayou, and on her cheek,
the urgent rasp of Spanish moss that beards

the wetland Cypresses; sees he has strewn
her bed with Mardi Gras beads, the sparkle
of a million stones, a lagniappe to tempt her;
a little more for a little less before pay-time.

She lies down among fake gems that spike
the hollow between her shoulder blades,
imprint themselves—listens
for the vodun drums—for his step.

Soul Food

In a separate pot, take Collard Greens,
boil them long and hard with salt.
and know they will keep their bright
aggressive colour, remain *al dente*.
Add potatoes, a red skinned variety,
to bubble alongside.

Once the water is reduced, combine
with ham from Wholefood Heaven,
pre-cut in blush-pink cubes of flesh.

Sauté green onions and garlic in butter
mixed with extra virgin olive oil.

Serve steaming hot with lashings
of Creole pepper; good the first day,
better the second, perfect the third—
mmmmm—over an open fire, bubbling
outside the cabins—slave food—

we eat it at home with gourmet
add-ons—feed our souls.

Definitions from the Katrina Pictionary
Waterworlds, A Katrina Pictionary, by Jan Gilbert and Deborah Howell

I am welcomed with tissues
in unopened boxes
essential in your too-recent
watery world

after the flood you say left your city
as if an atom bomb
had been dropped
no sounds of life

no sounds no birds singing
or the hum of wings
your *Waterloo*
the decisive defeat

by water in your home
in your road
where every other house
is spanking new

or boarded up
where *water rights*
are defined as the right
of water to transgress

any boundary
damage any property
in your home
where *waterworks*

is the shedding of tears
where your mother could pull
tissues from sleeves
like rabbits from hats

in your home
where mountains
of handkerchiefs
cannot stem the tide.

Abuelita,

little grandmother, has survived Katrina,
though terra cotta makes her vulnerable.

She holds her vigil in the living room
of my hostess—her splurge—

a chance to delight in the unaffordable.
Stark naked and unashamedly ancient,

she comes up to my shoulder, is missing
one arm, which could increase

her vulnerability, but lends her power
instead; an arm not lost to Katrina,

because a sculptor created her that way.
She smiles into my camera lens,

brandishes the stump of her never-needed
arm, a blissful half-smile—a two-arms-good-

one-arm-better smile, but her dreadlocks,
erect as misplaced phalluses, poke defiance

at the efforts of mortals to reconstruct her world.
They add to her height by inches.

Patchworking

I'm mending her quilt
a gaudy Katrina survivor,
its appliquéd squares
of cotton and cheesecloth
wearing out, wearing through
the seams slipping,
their stitches parting
from the near-transparent fabric
of old dresses stitched
into a web of former lives
worn tenderly
by frugal women
then consigned
to generational ragbags.

Mending her quilt
is a conversation about ancestors,
not always her own—
about hands that have come to the rescue
threading a tactful needle-path
up and down calico rows
where pink centres make
a cheeky nod to polka dots
while a bold stripe
takes up a floral challenge—
is taunted by geometrics
or a sudden shift in theme.

Some metaphors are inescapable
chase you down backstreets
like the deluge from a levee break
threaten to turn into cliché.
Over time these seams will shift
and gape, the threads
weaken and break.
The fabric will fray
where my clumsy stitches fail
and irreparable holes will appear—
cry out for darning,
for another pair of hands—
the lost art
of mending the unmendable.

Pelican Afternoon

Brown pelicans make a point of their own,
flap back robust as resurrection fern
fresh as miracles after heavy rain; dropped
in to command the afternoon, a return
to the spot where slavers might have docked,
set up their auction blocks, displayed their wares.
Crumbling walls and the moss of decay mark
their departure, a scene set for despair.

Survivors of Katrina's poisoned water,
the pelicans scoop and dip, nod their heads,
turn a blind eye to the decadent Quarter,
drowsy Creole girls curled up in their beds.
When the afternoon sun is warm and kind,
lovers rejoice in being colour blind.

Potter's Field, New Orleans-Style

We owe respect to the living, to the dead we owe only truth — Voltaire

Peeling paint, tilted headstones and bones
left by Katrina — vertebrae, fingers,
jaw fragments in the dirt, but we could
say they know how to bury their dead.

Black-crayoned letters spell out —
we miss you Mama, and next-door
The Jackson family, with a ragged list
of names and dates, added as required.

A baby lies nearby under a battered pram,
a pink rattle hanging from the hood,
while someone's son provides his mother
with a deck chair, surrounds her plot

with a picket fence. Here in Holt the dead
live on, cosseted by the care of the living
who hold umbrellas up to shield them
from rain, picnic above them on Sundays,

allow children to run free over their heads,
bring paint to freshen faded lettering
or drawings, secure in the knowledge
that the best graffiti is new and true.

The Banality of Rain

Is there no rain that is not cliché?
Torrential downpour
cats and dogs
nice weather for ducks
sheeting lashing
April showers
refreshing
rain-soaked
your archetypal
wet weekend.

The rain that raineth every day—
every life into which
a little rain must fall
come hell or high water
or even, when it rains it pours
which may mean
you either sink or swim.

Right as rain
wrong as rain
monsoon   hurricane
Katrina doesn't answer—
though Gustav's more restrained
and this time,
the levees hold.

Miceál Kearney

In the Pursuit of Happiness

I have been invited to a social gathering
in the Galway City Museum.
Hate these office-politics-sponsored events
Nobody knows I'm hiding,
high above them
in the Martin Oliver hooker.

It is lonely up here.
I can see her below —
laughing, mingling with the waves.
Starboard side
the smashing Atlantic
held at bay.

She makes me want to talk
mix and mingle, cast my vote
and God how I want to tell her.
My tongue ready, set
in concrete.

Reality dawns beneath
the drawn purple drapes.
Day creeps along the carpet.
Cruel light divides us equally.
Vampires — the night is ours

I still have time —
it's not yet now.
I watch you sleep,
start a new collection of poetry
called *Pi*.

It's something truly fantastic,
secretly held love —
pure heroin in virgin veins.

We came out in McDonagh's Fish and Chip shop.
Held hands above the table.
And lips. Some of them diners
couldn't care. Others said *Uh…*
and finished off their Haggis.

On the wooden armchair
I've often not wrote about.
1962, the uncle carved in school
brought home on his back
on his bike: placed in the kitchen
and hasn't moved since. Tonight
I surf sitting humble
on this rich piece of timber
and (according to my internet provider)
I have 1 unread message
from Bubblez_86.
Synapses surge through my body —

We have been emailing for months.
She told me she liked strawberry cheese cake
and the first book she read,
Crime and Punishment —
I RE:ed and told her
how I cried when the horse
was beaten to death.
The email opens,
and OMG, it's a date.

I wait and wonder nervously
how you'll have your hair.
A few months later, after the news
Crime Watch recalls with the aid of an actor:
my last known movements.

Sharon Black

Motherland

after the painting, Firth of Clyde, by Isis Olivier

Breakwater

In the middle of a gallery
I've wandered into to avoid the rain
in a smart Parisian *quartier,*
I find you wanton and dreaming,

reclining in the Firth of Clyde,
naked but for the isle of Arran
knuckled across your right breast, the dark mole
of Ailsa Craig midway down your *linea alba,*

a faint track of scars marking
underwater contours
and a single score of latitude. Your belly
skims the Ayrshire coastline,

its stretch marks catching in the sun
like silvery eels;
your pubic thatch is a shoal of fish
tugging on the current.

Both nipples are adrift—one nudging
the gentile seaside town of Troon,
the other its own unmapped island
cocked towards Kintyre.

Elbow thrown back
above your tipped-back head, fist
plunging the depths of Loch Fyne,
the Sound of Jura in your ears,

you hold back tides and wait,
warm as stone,
for rusting herring trawlers and the lonely nets
of wind-beaten fishermen.

Sepia

Hard to tell where body ends and land begins:
this coastline mapped in tendons and arteries,
in erogenous zones and stretch-marks,
your moon-curves pushing back landslide, bays and cliffs,
these wrinkled, flaking edges
that could crumble
like parchment under my hands.

Pilgrim

Mother, I trace your outline,
these ragged inlets, the crags and curves
that lead towards the Clyde;
how many miles, how many pilgrim miles
until we all come safely home?

Strand

You wear your body like a scroll,
your past laid out in nautical miles,
your present etched
with grid coordinates, latitude, place
names I've never heard of,
each muscle tensed, each sinew pushed
proud of Earth's crust, pectorals pulled
tight as a footbridge
I've been waiting on the other side of for years.

The Muse

I can't make out the islands' names,
their shaded clusters, but I manage
to map your nipples—
erect, peat-brown, ringed with tides—
am able to locate your pubic mound
in the mid-North Channel.

I angle thumb against parchment, squint,
count the widths from breast to coastline
to situate your heart.

I find it plum on Lady Isle—
'an island off the south Ayrshire coast,
uninhabited but for a lighthouse,
not the standard round-tower type
but a platform built on buttresses
with an exterior stairwell.

Today it is a bird sanctuary
and (despite the lighthouse) a popular place
for recreational sailors to run aground'.

Resting Place

They're out there searching still.
I hear the whirr of helicopter blades,
the churn of speedboats;
I know my loved ones are scanning
the cliffs below these coastal footpaths
while divers sweep their flashlights
like miniature lighthouses.

They will find no sailor here tonight.

For I have returned to peat, granite, brine.
Soon the Atlantic will flood my veins,
my outline will have risen
as a livid scar of coastline
and the dust of me will have slipped below sand.
I shift to make myself comfortable
as the tide sucks me flesh-wards.

Sam Adams

First Emperor

Thomas Herbert Esq. will visit the court of Jahangir, great grandson of Babur.
The Mughal Empire will flourish magnificently for two hundred years. The last
Emperor will be deposed by the British in 1857, following the Indian Mutiny.

1626   Lahore

In *Lahore* are many things observable—
The castle is large, strong, uniform,
pleasant, and bravely featured;
of stone, white, hard, and polished,
arm'd with twelve Posterns.
Within, a Palace sweet and lovely,
entred by two gates and Courts.

On the wall are pictur'd
sundry stories and pastimes, viz.
Iangheer (otherwise call'd *Sha Selym*)
croslegd upon a rich carpet,
under a stately throne or State,
his sonnes *Perwees* on the right hand,
And on the left hand,
Rajea Bousing fly-skarer,
Rajea Randas sword-bearer,
Mocrib-Chan Parasite,
Radjea Rodorow rebel.
In another, the Kings Progenitors,
of whom, *BABUR*,
& thirty nobles in the habit of Pilgrim Kalenders

(from *Some Yeares Travels into Divers Parts of Asia Afrique.*
by *Tho: Herbert. Esq. 1638*)

1483   Babur

Snow undulates along the valley floor,
and laps at the walls of Andijan.
Cherry trees raise bare arms
beseechingly; winter stings.
Guards at the palace gates
muffle mouths and nostrils,
stamp their feet. Beyond the distant
gleaming pinnacles of mountains,
above passes crupper-deep,
low in the night sky,
blazes a point of light: *Suhail*,
Canopus—star of good omen.

In the palace harem, by torchlight,
careful women stoop to gather up
the newborn child:
What a head, what shoulders ...
Go—go tell the king he has a son.

1484   The rider gives his message:
Yunus Khan, Lord of Samarkand
approaches.
             Omar Shaikh shifts
uneasily, inserts a marker
and slides the Book of Kings
beneath the richly bound Qur'an.

This he knew. A breeze travelling
east along the valley, Ferghana
prinking now for Spring, carried
drumbeats and again the shrill of pipes
far before the cavalcade.

Yunus Khan is late. The birthday
of his grandson, Zahir-ad-Din
Muhammad, has already passed;
the boy's head has been shaved,
its weight of hair in gold distributed
among the poor. Affairs of state—
how hold the clans, and keep
his head—have held him longer
than he thought or wished.

The child is naked, kicking
on a bed of fur laid on cloth of gold.
He clutches the proffered finger,
tugs it mouthwards. Yunus Khan
would take his hand away;
the small grasp tightens. *Allah be praised,
what monster have we here? We shall call him
Babur, Tiger,* says the Lord of Samarkand,
smiling at the mother. *You have
made us a true sprig of Genghis Khan.*

1488   The King of Ferghana must beg
peace of Samarkand. He rides
with retinue and son and heir.
Beneath his Mogul cap,
back straight, reins in one hand,
astride a wooden saddle,
he and the horse already one,
Babur is a smaller image
of his father—though not so fat.

Omar Shaikh is fat, and wary.
The old man, Yunus Khan,
is dead: Sultan Ahmed
rules Samarkand and eyes
the fertile valley of Ferghana—

as he would a comely woman
who, he knows, will drop
like ripe fruit should he but reach
out. So much for brotherly love.

From Uncle Ahmed, Babur receives
a child bride, and thinks,
What has this to do with me?
His eyes are full of wonders—
of blue-tiled domes gleaming in the sun,
and, in a pleasure garden, decked
with paintings of Mogul horsemen
putting battle-elephants of Hind
to flight, the tomb of Timur,
his father's great ancestor.

1495   Babur has a tutor. What, then, has he learned?
Of—Islam, numbers and poetry, the night sky
and its stars, the story of his family
from the time of Timur,
his four-times-great grandfather.
What language does he speak?
Chagatai Turkish—of soldiers who guard him
and tillers of fields who bring him melons,
pomegranates, grapes,
apricots stuffed with almonds;
the base Persian of traders in city streets;
the fine Persian and Arabic of learned men
and poets. He has begun to love books
and write poetry. He has learned to fight
with bow and sabre from the saddle
of a swiftly moving horse.

Omar Shaikh, who can fell a man
with one blow, plays tric-trac, drinks wine,
reads his favourite books. His fat swells
and bulges beneath the tightly-stretched
silk of his buttoned coat. Yet even now
he dreams the defeat of an older brother
and sees himself filling the throne
Of shining Samarkand.

                        But what ambition
he possessed has crumbled — drowned rather.
Content for him is talking
to his doves. He calls each
by name and when in turn they come,
he gently rubs the feathered breast,
whispering confession: *I am just,*
I think, and generous, but a sinner, too:
I gamble, I drink wine — often. I read
the Book of Kings, when I should study
the Qur'an. The plump bird coos.

Omar Shaikh has dovecotes
at all his dwellings in Ferghana.
and in summer visits each. At Akhsi,
where the castle perches watchful
on a perilous height above river
and town, the cote hangs partly out
over the cliff wall of a deep ravine.
With blessings for his birds and seed
their master enters: the doves flock in.
Who knows which last bird entering,
which feather falling tipped the scale?
With a wrenching of ancient timbers,
the dovecote tilts. Fat Omar Shaikh slides
Backwards.

           Looking up, dazed
workers in the fields beheld
a prodigy — a dovecote falling,

tumbling in the air, birds bursting out
like shrapnel, and then heard
the splintering crash on river rocks.
At twelve, Babur is king of Ferghana...

1501   At eighteen, Lord of Samarkand,
holding the city walls against
an Uzbek horde. The siege
is long: horses feed on wood chips
soaked in water, before becoming food.
Babur has a tiger's strength
(can raise and hold a man
beneath each arm and run with them
along a parapet) —and courage.
He sleeps in chain mail,
leads against a host his loyal handful;
At last, alone and desperate, survives by flight.
The Little Father of Physicians
heals his wounds with dried fruit skins
wrapped in the pelt of a fox's leg...

1505   At twenty-three, King of Kabul.
Of Kabul? Six hundred miles away?
How comes that?
Honoured still as Timur's youthful heir,
he draws, hardly knowing how,
another army to him, but not to face
the Uzbeks. He leaves his homeland,
turning south towards the Hindu Kush.
Threading a high pass
among the towering pinnacles,
for the first time he sees,
low in a purple sky, *Suhail*,
bright star of good omen and, with daylight,
in a great bowl of mountains,
Qabil, the Land of Cain.

The citadel above the river surrenders
without fight. He rules
from mountains to desert sands,
where wind among the dunes
drums the hoof-beats of ghostly armies.

One by one he brings the Afghan
warlords, with grass between their teeth,
to heel, and begins to plant himself anew.
He must have gardens with watercourses,
Fruitful orchards, spreading plane trees,
Beneath which he can read,
And write the story of his life.
He is a warrior at rest in the shade.

1506   Winter on the plains, winter
along old caravan roads: nothing
moves. Opposing armies,
Winter breathing in their faces,
dissolve and dwindle
to their homes.
                    Babur, tiring
of princely cousins' revels
in Herat, and anxious for Kabul,
gathers his remaining men
and points them to the mountains—
due east, the lowest pass
ten thousand feet.
                    Cold crackles
in the mountains. Summer torrents
Are thick-ribbed cataracts of ice;
obliterating snow has crept down
every rocky fold and scree.
All too easily the guide
strays from the well-known path,
and they are lost, packed snow
to the riders' stirrups. The horses, blind,
would bolt, but cannot move.

In turn the men dismount, pushing
against the wall, trampling it down,
leading their horses forward
and upward, yard by yard, day by day.
Toes and fingers blacken.
A blizzard wipes out
their snaking path behind.
The shortest day is endless.
High on a ridge, a crack in the rock
promises shelter for a few. *Go in, go in,*
They call above the gale, but Babur,
King, will share the misery of those
outside, *Death in the midst of friends*
is a feast, he quotes aloud to no one.
He digs a space in the endless white,
sits there until prayer time, while falling snow
covers head and back and ears
four fingers deep.
                    Suddenly a voice:
We have been deeper – this cave
has room enough for everyone.
From ice nests they struggle up
and stumble in. What little food
remains is shared by all. Limbs thaw;
in fiery agony feeling returns.
They sleep.
                    Two days, two more dreadful days
of cold, bring them to a village—warm houses,
boiled mutton, hay and corn for the horses,
Wood and dried dung for fires.
And two days more, Kabul.

1525   Broad from snowmelt, Kabul River
            flows east and south to join the mighty Indus.
            Babur eyes the glistening pathway
            in the summer sun and ponders
            his Timurid destiny.

149

It is winter once more; his army,
advances over Khyber: twelve thousand men
and for the first time cannon and matchlocks
with trained Turks to aim them.

1526   At Panipat, the legions of Delhi,
battle elephants before, are overcome,
as they were by Timur,
the Sultan killed. Babur posts
Prince Humayun, his son, with all speed,
to the treasury at Agra. He orders prayers
and charity in his name, as *Padishah*,
Emperor of Kabul and Delhi.

Does he then enter his new realm
In triumph and revel in its riches?
No. Koh-i-Nur, the great diamond
Taken at Agra, he gives back to his son;
the wealth of the Delhi treasury
he divides among his soldiers,
content, it's said, to take himself
a beggar's share. He thus becomes
The Kalandar King.

1531   Babur has matched his men against
the best of Hindustan. Rajput warriors,
famed through all the world,
having fled the field, disgraced,
kill one another in ritual sacrifice.
Babur would have spared them—
he is merciful to enemies who come
contrite before him. He is not a pillager,
he does not despoil.
           At rest once more,
he looks about his new domain,
but with distaste, and a will to change what he
                     sees.

Where he can he builds and beautifies
the steaming plain—and hungers for the

                                   mountains,
for Kabul.

Unlike Timur, he plans to stay.
Humayun, his eldest son, heir to two kingdoms,
is reminded of the duties of kingship
and called back from Kabul. Ever restless
beneath his father's gaze,
the Prince comes to Agra.

Babur suffers that affliction
of the bowels that has so often been
a dread companion on campaigns,
defeated, like his enemies, it seems by will.
Then Humayun, reluctant
princely prentice of his father,
falls foul of the bloody flux.
Life drains away, his body wastes,
the watching women weep.
From his own sick bed Babur rises
to attend his son. Physicians
shake their heads: *My Lord, your son
is beyond our care. Then go*, he answers,
go. I shall trust to God's providence.

In the terrible heat of the day, he slowly circles
his son's couch, *Oh, God, if a life
may be taken for a life, I who am Babur,
I give my life and my being
for that of my son, Humayun.*
Ever more slowly he moves, ever more feebly
his prayer ascends. As the sun burns
Jumna waters dark red, the Emperor falls.
With great care attendants lift
and bear him away.

Humayun stirs.
Water is brought, he is bathed ...
He rises.

It is late in the year again. The days
of great heat and rain have passed,
but for Babur there is no relief from flux,
from fever. His face shrinks; great bones stretch
the parchment of his skin. The doctors
despair. He calls on all to acknowledge
Humayun his heir, and on Humayun
to be faithful to his brothers
and all his people.
                    The women return to the palace,
each to find a corner and weep alone;
Suhail, Canopus hides his bright head.

1540   According to his last wishes,
              the remains of Babur, *Padishah*,
              removed from Agra, are buried
              in Kabul. On his tomb, amidst flowers,
              in the shade of trees, a line
              of Persian is inscribed:
              If there is paradise on earth,
              it is this, it is this, it is.

Bruce Ackerley is 43, lives and works in Nottingham as a Local Government Housing Officer. He has been writing for the better part of a decade, having published two collections of poetry, to date: *Sound of Mountain*, with Cinnamon Press in 2006 and *Nantyr Sequence*, with Triskele in 2009.

Sam Adams – poet, novelist and critic. His third book of poems, *Missed Chances*, was published in 2007, and his novel *Prichard's Nose* in 2010, both by Y Lolfa. He contributes a regular 'Letter from Wales' to the Carcanet magazine *Pn Review*.

Andrew Bailey was one of the original editors for the Poetry Archive, and has also worked for the Poetry Society, Poetry International Web and a handful of fringe theatre companies. Poems have appeared widely, online and offline, in journals including Poetry Review, The Rialto, Ambit, Brittle Star, Gists and Piths and Stand. He was the 2005 winner of the Geoffrey Dearmer Prize. A collection, Zeal, is forthcoming from Enitharmon.

Peter Barry has had poems in *Poetry Wales, New Welsh Review,* and *Stand* over the past few years, and is a member of the Aberystwyth University Poetry Workshop. He attended St Joseph's College (at Upholland, Lancs.) in the 1960s, and then King's College, London, moving, in effect, from the monastic regime of the fourteenth century to Swinging London. He is now Professor of English at Aberystwyth.

Ruth Bidgood was born of a North Welsh father and a West Country mother in Seven Sisters, Glamorgan. Educated Port Talbot and Oxford University, in the 60s, after many years away (in Oxford, Alexandria and the London area) she returned to Wales and settled in Powys, where she began writing poetry and local history. Her eighth collection of poems was published by Seren in 2000: the second received a Welsh Arts Council award; the sixth and seventh were shortlisted for the Welsh Arts Council Book of the Year Award in 1993 and 1997. Her latest collection, Time Being, was a Poetry Society Recommendation and won the 2011 Roland Mathias Prize.

Sharon Black is originally from Glasgow but now lives in the remote Cévennes mountains of southern France. In her former life she was a journalist, in her current one she organises holiday courses including creative writing courses (www.gardoussel.com) and teaches English to 7-8 year-old French kids. She especially enjoys sharing her knowledge of traditional Scottish songs – educational standards such as Ye Cannae Shove yer Granny aff a Bus. Sushi, dancing and the music of Dar Williams (not all at the same time) are among her passions.

Alison Brackenbury's latest collection is *Singing in the Dark*, (Carcanet , 2008). A selection of new poems can be seen on her website, www.alisonbrackenbury.co.uk

Anne Cluysenaar was born Belgium in 1936 and studied at Trinity College, Dublin, taking Irish citizenship in 961. She lives in Wales. Among her publications are *Nodes* (Dolmen Press, 1971), *Double Helix* (Carcanet,1982); new and selected poems, *Timeslips* (Carcanet, 1997); *Batu-Angas: Envisioning Nature with Alfred Russell Wallace* (Seren, 2008); autobiographical poems, *Water to Breathe* (Flarestack, 2009). Selected poems from her 'Vaughan Variations' (*Timeslips*) are included in *Poetry 1900 - 2000, One hundred poets from Wales*, ed. Meic Stephens (Parthian, 2007). *Migrations* is forthcoming with Cinnamon Press in 2011.

Tony Curtis is Professor of Poetry at the University of Glamorgan where he set up Creative Writing in the early 1980s. He has published nine collections, the latest of which was *Crossing Over* (Seren, 2007) and had just written *Real South Pembrokeshire* for the same press. His *The Meaning of Apricot Sponge: John Tripp Selected Writings* was published recently.

Lee Duggan was born in London in 1976 and moved to North Wales in 1996 where she found home with her two daughters and dog. In the final stages of an MA in Creative Writing at Bangor University, she is currently working towards her first collection with Salt. As a Forest School leader and keen walker, being part of the outdoor environment drives her creativity alongside more formal approaches to writing.

Rebecca Gethin's first collection, *River is the Plural of Rain*, was published by Oversteps Books in 2009 and she has read her poems both in London and Devon, on local radio and on television. She is currently a tutor of creative writing in a prison and occasionally runs workshops on the outside, too. Her first novel, *Lair Dice*, is to be published by Cinnamon Press in 2011.

Daphne Gloag was a medical journalist and editor after reading classics and philosophy. Her second collection, A *Compression of Distances* (Cinnamon Press, 2009), includes part of Beginnings, a long poem with a cosmological setting that is still the focus of her work. Her prizes include first prize for a Poetry on the Lake competition and for the last Scintilla short poem competition. She was married to a poet, the late Peter Williamson.

Miceál Kearney is 30 and lives in the West of Ireland. Published in magazines and anthologies in Ireland, England and America, in 2009 he was selected to read at Poetry Ireland's Introductions Series and has won a few Poetry Grand Slams and was short-listed for the 2007 Cinnamon Press Poetry Collection Award. *Inheritance*, Miceál's debut collection was published in 2008 by Doire Press and he is currently working on his second collection, *Interest*.

Will Kemp studied at Cambridge and UEA, then travelled throughout Asia and South America, before working as an environmental planning consultant in Holland, Canada and New Zealand. He won the *Envoi International Poetry Competition* in 2010, and has had poems published in various national journals. He has been shortlisted for the Cinnamon Poetry Award four times and his first collection, *Nocturnes*, is forthcoming with Cinnamon Press.

Wendy Klein is a retired psychotherapist living in a deceptively elegant Victorian apartment in the Berkshire countryside. Winner of the Ware Poetry Competition (2009) and the Torriano Competition (2010), her first collection, *Cuba in the Blood* was published by Cinnamon Press in February 2009, and second is due out in early 2013. Her most recent work, in tandem with the Swedish translator, Jan Teeland, is a book-length single poem by the Swedish poet, Helena Erickson, which has just been accepted by Shearsman Press.

Pete Marshall was born in Liverpool in 1958. He has worked at many occupations, from a soldier to a social worker. His writing appears regularly in literary magazines and his first collection was published by the Frogmore Press in 1989. His second collection, *In Loco Parentis,* explores child abuse and children in care was and his third collection, *The Vale*, was written during a six months writer's sabbatical in the Vale of Glamorgan. His collection *AGOG* is forthcoming from Cinnamon Press. Pete is married with three children and lives on a traditional Welsh smallholding in the Conwy Valley.

Susan Richardson is a poet, performer and educator whose first collection, *Creatures of the Intertidal Zone*, was inspired by her journey through Iceland, Greenland and Newfoundland in the footsteps of an intrepid eleventh century female Viking. She is one of the poets-in-residence on BBC Radio 4's 'Saturday Live' and has also been commissioned to write and perform poetry for BBC 2's coverage of the Chelsea Flower Show. Susan's next collection, *Where the Air is Rarefied*, a collaboration with a visual artist, is recently published by Cinnamon Press. www.susanrichardsonwriter.co.uk

Sue Rose is a literary translator and poet whose work has appeared in a variety of magazines and anthologies. In 2009, she won the prestigious Troubadour Poetry Prize and, in 2008, the Canterbury Festival Poet of the Year Competition. She has also been commended or placed in competitions such as the National, the Peterloo and the Wigtown. Her debut collection, *From the Dark Room*, is forthcoming with Cinnamon Press in 2011.

Myra Schneider's recent poetry collections are *Multiplying The Moon* (Enitharmon 2004) and *Circling The Core* (Enitharmon 2008). Other books include *Writing My Way Through Cancer* (Jessica Kingsley 2003) and *Writing Your Self* (with John Killick) (Continuum 2009). Myra was shortlisted for a Forward Prize in 2007, is a tutor for The Poetry School, has co-edited four anthologies of poetry by contemporary women poets and is consultant to the Second Light Network of women poets.

Derek Sellen, now a teacher in Canterbury, has lived in Madrid and Salamanca, where he first encountered a range of Spanish art. 'A Guide to the Spanish Painters' developed over several months and led to discoveries of works and painters new to him, such as Angeles Santos, as well as re-acquaintance with powerful images by El Greco, Miro, Gris and others. The first five poems of the sequence were published in *Storm at Galesburg* (Cinnamon Press).

N S Thompson was born in Manchester and moved to Italy in his twenties, then to Oxford in his thirties for a brief academic career. His latest work is a long poem *Letter to Auden* (Smokestack, 2010) in rime royal, an analysis by turns comic and serious of the contemporary world.

Ruth Thompson lives in Belfast, Northern Ireland, and is a graduate of Queen's University MA in Creative Writing. Her work appears in a range of anthologies and publications, including *THE SHOp* and *Southlight Magazine*. She received the Bluechrome Writers' Award for Poetry in 2007, participated in Poetry Ireland's 2009 'Introductions Series', and is a commended prizewinner in the 2010 Wigtown Poetry Prize.

Bonnie Thurston lives quietly in her home state, West Virginia after thirty years as a university professor. Author or editor of fifteen theological books and many articles, her poetry appears frequently in periodicals. Two collections were published by Three Peaks Press, Wales: *The Heart's Lands* and *Hints and Glimpses*. In 2011 Liturgical Press releases *Belonging to Borders*, Bonnie's poems in the Celtic tradition.

Susan Utting is a Peterloo Prize poet whose latest collection, *Houses Without Walls* (Two Rivers Press) was featured in the *Independent on Sunday* and included in the *Forward Book of Poetry*, Best Poem category. New work has recently appeared in the *TLS, The North, The Daily Mirror* (Carol Anne Duffy's choice) and was selected by *The Times* for its Best Love Poem 2010 showcase.

Nicola Warwick was born in Kent and now lives and works in Suffolk. She has had poems in several magazines, including *The Rialto, Smiths Knoll* and *Magma*. She has also received commendations in competitions and as a result her work has appeared in various anthologies. She is currently at work on her first collection and hopes to find a home for it soon.